THE BEST OF
Swedish Cooking

DAILY FARE AND
FESTIVE DISHES FROM
THE TEST KITCHEN OF
THE SWEDISH AGRICULTURAL
ORGANISATIONS

Natur och Kultur

Photo
Ulf Christer pp 11, 14, 18, 24, 55, 57, 66, 76,
82, 85, 95, 98, 103, 128, 135, 136, 139, 143,
155, 164, 169, 172
Lars Paulsson pp 15, 17, 22, 28, 31, 33, 35,
45, 49, 51, 59, 63, 65, 72, 79, 91, 106, 109,
114–115, 120, 123, 125, 129, 148–149, 160,
162, 167, 170, 173

Editor: Stina Algotson

Cover design: Per E Lindgren

Translation: Mona Øksbro

© 1983 Jordbrukets Provkök and LTs Förlag
© 1995 Jordbrukets Provkök and Bokförlaget Natur och Kultur
AB Boktryck, Helsingborg 1995 (1:3)
ISBN 91-27-05483-7

Contents

Preface

The Test Kitchen of the Swedish Agricultural Organizations started its operations 20 years ago, its purpose to promote good cooking through stimulating, by various means, the interest for food and cooking, chiefly using Swedish farm products. The Test Kitchen is jointly owned by The Swedish Dairy Association, The Swedish Farmers' Meat Marketing Association, The Swedish Farmers' Supply & Crop Marketing Organization, and the Swedish Egg Marketing Association.

Over the years the Test Kitchen has accumulated a large collection of recipes. Commissioned by the owners and other co-operative farming enterprises the Test Kitchen has compiled material for pamphlets and articles, and much work has gone into text and illustrations. All recipes are prepared, tasted and discussed, and all dishes to be illustrated are prepared for photography in the Test Kitchen's studio.

In order to preserve the value of this work, we have now collected the recipes which are most in demand, most appreciated and traditional to be published in book form.

The recipes were compiled and edited by home economist *Stina Algotson*, who was employed with the Test Kitchen for nearly nine years and who is now a freelance journalist. In co-operation with the Test Kitchen she has evaluated the prepared dishes, particularly the ingredients, proportions, cooking methods, flavour, and consistency.

Stina Algotson has arranged the illustrations in co-operation with the photographer *Lars Paulsson*. He has been working in close co-operation with the Test Kitchen since its start and he is known as one of the best food photographers in Sweden.

The introductory chapter about Swedish food traditions was written by curator Gunilla Englund.

It is our hope that "The Best of Swedish Cooking" will lead many to discover the Swedish food traditions.

The Test Kitchen of the Swedish Agricultural Organizations

Introduction

TO THE ENGLISH EDITION

Swedish traditional cooking was developed regionally, using local raw materials, at a time when few if any imported products were available. It has been developed over many generations, adopting and absorbing outside influences on its way, so that it now includes a rich variety of dishes, which are tasty, wholesome, and characteristic of the Swedish climate and culture.

During the last thirty years the traditional Swedish cooking has been pushed into the background by a multitude of more or less ready-cooked products of standardized content and flavour. New ingredients have been imported, especially vegetables, fruit, and herbs.

Swedish traditional cooking, however, deserves not only to be preserved within Sweden, but also to be known by a wider public. When this book was published in Sweden, it was greeted with enormous interest and demands for an English translation. It gives a picture of genuine Swedish cooking, both plain and fancy, and outlines its cultural background. Thus "The Best of Swedish Cooking" is of value to those having a personal interest in Sweden, as well as to those interested in international cooking for purely gastronomic reasons.

The recipes are based on traditional Swedish food, using modern cooking methods and ingredients. Swedes like their food to be good and well cooked. The cooking is based on principles concerned with drawing out the flavour of the basic ingredient and with preserving the nutritive value of the food. You will find that the cooking methods are simple and straight forward and the ingredients of each recipe are few and well matched.

The combination of ingredients is sometimes surprising. One typically Swedish trick is to bring out a savoury flavour by adding a sweetening agent such as redcurrant jelly, treacle (molasses), or a pinch of sugar. Nowadays this method has caught on in many countries, but in Sweden it has been used for generations.

It is not difficult to prepare Swedish dishes in your own kitchen. The ingredients are mostly familiar ones, easily obtainable everywhere, and those which are not can often be found in delicatessen shops. On the following pages I have indicated some ingredients, which give Swedish dishes their distinctive flavour and texture and described in what whay the Swedish use of them may differ from their use in other countries. In a few cases, where the ingredients may be difficult or even impossible to find outside Sweden, I have suggested substitutes, which will not change the essential character of the dish.

The translator

Swedish food

A BRIEF HISTORICAL BACKGROUND by Gunilla Englund

A foreign visitor who is introduced to Swedish food today may be served the following delicacies: herring and potatoes, marinated salmon, reindeer-roast, cured leg of mutton, fermented Baltic herring, or crayfish. All these dishes were once daily fare in different parts of Sweden. Many of the so called regional dishes originated in a particular region because of its climate and nature.

Sweden used to be a self-sufficient society. Each household had to produce its own food and very little was purchased. Salt was a vitally important commodity, which could not be produced at home. Salt was essential for the preservation of meat and fish.

Sweden is a long country with a varied climate. This dictated to a great extent what could be cultivated in the different parts of the country. Flatbread became the typical bread of Norrland, because barley tolerates the cold climate. Barley, however, rises badly, therefore the bread became thin and flat.

The daily fare was monotonous. The most common dishes were gruel, porridge, herring, salted bacon (salt pork), soup, cabbage, peas, potatoes, and bread. As most provisions had to be stored for a long time, fresh food was rarely served. In the autumn stores had to be laid up for a whole year.

Large catches of fish had to be prepared for extended storage. To preserve the fish, it was either salted, dried, fermented, or marinated. Fish to be marinated was salted in its own juice, packed in wooden barrels, and buried in the ground. Linné wrote about this fish that it smelt bad, was red around the bones, but was considered a delicacy. Much of the fish was dried. Nowadays dried fish is eaten only at Christmas: the traditional *lutfisk* (dried ling or cod, pickled in lye). In some parts of the country, where bread was scarce, dried fish spread with dripping had to replace it.

Bread was the mainstay of the diet before the potato arrived. Different kinds of bread were baked throughout the country; in the South it was customary to bake soft loaves from rye, in Central Sweden crisp bread. The hole in the middle of the crisp bread remains from the time when the bread was hung from the ceiling to dry. In Norrland, flatbread was baked from barley. Even the bread had to last a long time. Baking was usually done twice a year, at Christmas and Midsummer. Too frequent baking was a sign of poverty. Bread played an important part at feasts, this can be seen from the variety of shapes of bread baked, which depended on the feast in question. Old tradition required that in spring, at sowing time, a loaf from previous harvest be crumbled and scattered over the fields to ensure a good harvest. Crop failure usually meant famine.

Not even milk was consumed fresh; only infants and sick persons were allowed fresh milk. The milk was left in basins and later the cream was skimmed off to be used for making butter. The skim milk was used as a drink or served with porridge. The butter was usually sold or paid as tax. Porridge and gruel were important parts of the daily fare. The porridge played its role not only for everyday use, but was also served at many festive occasions. The expression, "to get into the butter", is connected with porridge. A lump of butter was sometimes placed in the middle of the porridge and one had to eat one's way to the butter. Whoever reached it first was said to have got into the butter. Childbirth, wedding, or housemoving were occasions for feast porridge. It was also called white porridge, as it was prepared with milk or cream; everyday porridge was prepared with water.

Soup was simple and satisfying, particularly the broth. Nowadays the only remnant of our soup tradition is the pea soup, which is eaten faithfully every Thursday.

The potato is said to have saved many lives in the 19th century, when crop failure was common and the population increased rapidly. The potato is a late arrival in the Swedish food tradition. It was known already in the 17th century, but significant cultivation only started in the 19th century. At the beginning it met with strong opposition. Only when it was discovered that the potato could replace grain in alcohol fabrication, did the interest for this new-fangled crop increase.

Before the potato, turnips and cabbage had to supplement the pork and the fish. Cabbage and onions were probably the earliest vegetables cultivated in Sweden. Peas and broad beans have been cultivated since ancient times. Peas were ground into flour when grain was in short supply. Vegetables were mainly cultivated at castles, manors, and abbeys, where new varieties were tried out.

Eggs belonged to spring and summer. The hens did not lay well in the darkness and cold of the winter. Feast recipes as pyramide cake and omelet contained a lot of eggs, just as the fine cake *gorån*. In spring eggs were also gathered from the nests of wild birds.

Fruit and berries were also part of the Swedish diet, especially lingonberries, blueberries, and cloudberries, which could be gathered in the woods. Lingonberries were very important. They were eaten with potatoes, porridge, and pancakes. They were cooked without sugar. Apples were grown on the farms and gooseberries and currants also have an old tradition in Sweden.

In order to make the provisions last for a whole year it was important to utilize all that could be eaten. Today we consider certain parts of an animal unfit for human consumption, but a good old housewife threw nothing away.

It the daily fare was monotonous, so much more was put on the table at the feasts. Wedding and funeral celebrations might go on for several days. The guests usually brought something to eat, a kind of surprise party.

Therefore it was important that everybody tasted all the dishes, so that none of the cooks should feel belittled.

One of the biggest feasts in the year was Christmas. All the larders were filled. Just for this once in the year, fresh food was served in abundance. It was important to show generosity at Christmas time, so people shared readily with those who were poor.

Swedish cookery has always been influenced by other countries. There has always been a certain immigration into Sweden. Then as now the immigrants brought their food traditions along. It is said that people's strongest habits are their eating habits. Many immigrants try to prepare their traditional dishes. If this is not possible every day, at least it is done at festive occasions.

Formerly new additions to the Swedish kitchen came mostly through castles and manors. In the 17th century, when Sweden was an important power, the German kitchen was in fashion. During Gustav III's reign the French kitchen was considered the foremost. The upper classes could afford to buy imported goods, for instance exotic spices and fruits. They also had the rights to hunt in the forests, something the farmers were generally not allowed. Thus, for those who could afford it, the possibilities to vary their diet were greatly increased.

Many of the traditional Swedish dishes are still with us. We no longer need to rely on year-old salted bacon (salt pork), sour milk, and turnips, but even so the Swedish everyday food is experiencing a renaissance in modernized form. Show me the Swede who does not, after a long stay abroad, speak lyrically about crisp bread and caviar. We are now used to having most raw materials in continuous supply throughout the year. But it is still exciting to follow the seasons with their various specialities, just as it was done not so long ago, before modern cold-storage and quick communications were available.

The Swedish store cupboard

This list is by no means exhaustive but it includes ingredients which are in frequent use in the Swedish kitchen, or whose inclusion in a meal will add a Swedish touch.

DRY GOODS

Flour For cooking plain white flour is used. For bread-making a wide choice of flour and crushed grain of wheat, rye, oats, and barley is available. In recent years several mixed flours have come on the market. Further details are given in the recipes. For cakes and biscuits plain flour and baking powder is used.

Potato Flour (potato starch) is often used as a thickening agent, especially in sweet sauces, fruit-soups, and creams. If potato flour is not available, corn flour (Am. corn-starch) may be used, but in that case the sauce or cream must be simmered a couple of minutes after the thickening has been added.

Dried Breadcrumbs are frequently used, for instance as a coating, in forcemeat, and in sweets. Mostly white breadcrumbs are used, only a few recipes, like Swedish Apple Cake, call for dark rye bread crumbs.

Sugar Unless otherwise specified, use granulated sugar.

Rice was rarely used in Swedish traditional cooking. The roundgrained type was used for porridge (especially Christmas porridge) and in stuffings and forcemeat. In recent years long-grained rice has come into use as an accompaniment to meat dishes, replacing potatoes.

BOTTLED AND TINNED GOODS

Anchovies of the Swedish type are really spiced cured sprats. They are used in various combinations with eggs and in the famous potato gratin "Jansson's Temptation". They are sold tinned (whole or filleted) and they are normally used without de-salting. If you cannot find Swedish anchovies, use anchovies in oil or salt herring.

Swedish Caviar is mostly sold in tubes. It is made from cod's roe, which is salted, puréed, and often smoked. Oil is added and sometimes dill. Swedish caviar is used in many dishes and it is highly appreciated on open sandwiches. It is rather difficult to find a substitute for but on sandwiches imported caviar may be substituted.

Swedish mustard is mild and rather sweet. A German-type mustard can be used as substitute.

Swedish Soy Sauce is a mixture of caramel colouring, soy extract and salt. It is used mainly as a colouring agent in sauces, soups and stews. Use caramel colouring as a substitute with a few drops of Chinese soy sauce added.

Vinegar Wine and cider vinegar are comparatively little used in Sweden. Alcohol vinegar, sold in different concentrations, is used diluted for pickling. In the recipes I have given proportions for 12 % essence of vinegar and for wine or cider vinegar. In USA regular white vineger may be used. In this case use the proportions given for essence of vineger.

Lingonberry Jam (red whortleberry jam) will supply the Swedish touch to many dishes. It is served with pancakes and many other desserts, but also as a sweet-sour accompaniment to meat. Don't worry if you cannot find it, cranberry sauce makes an excellent substitute.

VEGETABLES

Potatoes Plain boiled potatoes are most often served with everyday meat and fish dishes. There are, however, many interesting ways to prepare potatoes, as you will find in the chapter Potato Dishes.

Turnips (Swedes) are used, especially in winter, for mashed turnips and in casserole-dishes.

Soup Vegetables are normally carrots, parsnips, leeks, and celeriac (celery-root).

Mushrooms The Swedes eat many kinds of mushrooms, and they like going into the fields and forests to gather them. The most appreciated species are (apart from the champignons) chanterelles, morels, and boletus.

Onions Yellow onions are used in most of the dishes. For pickled herring and in some salads the large red variety (Copper King) is preferred.

Celeriac (celery-root) is used as an aromatic in soups and stews. Substitute celery, if you cannot find any celeriac.

Horseradish is highly appreciated in hot and cold sauces, with soured cream, and in some salads. It is also used as a preservative when pickling cucumbers or beetroots.

FRESH HERBS

Parsley, **dill**, and **chives** are used lavishly in Swedish cooking.
Thyme is also appreciated, especially in the yellow pea soup.

DRIED HERBS

Thyme, **marjoram**, and **bay leaves** are the most popular ones.
Juniper berries are used in many game dishes.

SPICES

Black and **white pepper** are often used interchangeably in the recipes.
Allspice, **cloves**, **cinnamon**, and **ginger** are used both whole and powdered.
Saffron is used in the traditional Christmas buns.
Vanilla is mostly replaced by vanilline sugar. In the recipes I have given proportions for vanilla extract as an alternative.

DAIRY PRODUCTS

Butter or margarine are normally used for frying and baking. Almost all butter sold in Sweden is lightly salted, so lightly that it can be used in cakes. Only a very small quantity is sold unsalted or extra salted.
Cream is an important ingredient in many recipes. It is used in sauces, soups, and as an accompaniment to many sweets. The Swedish whipping cream is equivalent to the English whipping cream (Am. heavy cream) with a butterfat content of 40 %. When cream is called for in a recipe, use single cream (12 %). The Swedish soured cream, *gräddfil*, has, just as its English counterpart, a butterfat content of 12 %.

MEASUREMENTS

Metric, imperial, and American measurements are given. When following a recipe, stick to one kind of measurement; do not mix them or the proportions might be wrong. All spoon and volume measurements are level. Some British terms may seem unfamiliar to the American readers. In such cases the American terms is given between brackets.

Porridge and gruel (Hot Cereals)

Porridge and gruel were everyday dishes in the old days and will even now provide cheap and easily prepared nourishment, morning as well as evening, when you have thousands of things to do apart from cooking.

Nowadays porridge has become a rare dish on the breakfast table. This is undoubtedly due to the increased consumption of cultured milk products like soured milk and yoghurt. Perhaps it is time to rediscover the hot gruel as breakfast on cold winter mornings.

Both porridge and gruel make excellent evening meals for those who have their main meal at midday.

Oatmeal Porridge 4 servings *Havregrynsgröt*

120 g/4 oz/1½ cup porridge oats
900 ml/good 1½ pts/3¾ cups water
1 tsp salt

Mix oatmeal, water, and salt in a saucepan. Bring to the boil and simmer gently while stirring for about 3 min.
Serve with milk and apple sauce or a fruit purée.

Variation: *Oatmeal Porridge with*   *Havregrynsgröt med äpple*
Apples
Core 2–3 apples and grate them coarsely. Proceed as described in the recipe above, but use only 800 ml (scant 1½ pts/3⅓ cups) water and ½ tsp salt. Mix all the ingredients in a saucepan and cook as above.
Serve with milk.

Semolina Porridge (Cream of Wheat) 4 servings *Mannagrynsgröt*

800 ml/scant 1½ pts/3¼ cups milk
½–1 tsp salt
90 g/3 oz/½ cup semolina

Bring the milk to the boil with the salt. Beat in the semolina. Simmer on low heat while stirring for 4–5 min.
Serve with milk and apple sauce or a fruit purée.

Variation: 'Klappgröt'
Replace the milk in the above recipe with 600 ml (1 pt/2½ cups) water and 200 ml (7 fl oz/good ¾ cup) undiluted fruit-syrup. Omit the salt and use only 70 g (2½ oz/scant ½ cup) semolina.
Bring water and fruit-syrup to the boil. Beat in the semolina. Simmer on low heat while beating for 4–5 min. Remove the saucepan from the heat and put it in a basin with cold water.
While the porridge is cooling, beat it vigorously, either with an electric beater or in your mixing machine.
Serve with milk.

A good breakfast gives you a good start.

Barley-, Rye- or Whole wheat Porridge (Cereal) 4 servings

Kornmjöls-, rågmjöls-, eller grahamsmjölsgröt

1 l/1¾ pts/4¼ cups water
1 tsp salt
300 ml/½ pt/1¼ cups barley, rye or
    whole wheat flour

Bring water and salt to the boil. Beat in the flour little by little. Simmer on low heat while stirring for about 5 min. Serve with milk and lingonberry jam or apple sauce.

Oatmeal Gruel 4 servings

Havrevälling

1 l/1¾ pts/4¼ cups milk
½–1 tsp salt
50 g/2 oz/⅔ cup oat meal
100 ml/3½ fl oz/scant ½ cup finely
    chopped prunes or raisins

Mix milk, salt, and oatmeal in a saucepan. Bring to the boil and simmer gently while stirring for about 3 min.
Add the prunes or raisins towards the end of the cooking-time.

Semolina Gruel (Cream of Wheat) 4 servings

Mannagrynsvälling

1 l/1¾ pts/4¼ cups milk
½–1 tsp salt
½ tbs butter
35 g/1¼ oz/scant ¼ cup semolina
30–60 g/1–2 oz/¼–½ cup raisins

Bring milk, salt, and butter to the boil in a saucepan. Beat in the semolina. Simmer on low heat while stirring for 4–5 min.
Add the raisins towards the end of the cooking-time.

Variation: *Wheat-flour Gruel (Cream of Wheat)* *Slätvälling*
Substitute 4 tbs wheat flour for the semolina in the above recipe. Mix the flour with a little of the cold milk. Bring the rest of the milk to the boil together with salt and butter. Beat in the flour mixture and simmer gently while stirring for 3–5 min.
Add raisins as above or flavour with 1–2 tbs sugar.

Everyday soups

The traditional everyday soups were often prepared in such a way that they could be used to dispose of leftovers. One lived after the principle that everything must be put to use. As the meat was normally boiled good broth was available, which, together with fresh or dried vegetables, made a good and satisfying dish.

With the supplies available today we can all the year round produce the good and wholesome soups, which formerly used to be seasonal specialities. We can enjoy Spring Vegetable Soup and Broad Bean Soup even in winter time, thanks to frozen vegetables.

Pea soup is one of the most popular ready-cooked dishes. But those who have prepared large quantities of home-cooked soup appreciate having a supply in the deep-freeze for Thursday dinners, which is the most common soup day in Sweden.

Meat and Vegetable Soup   4 servings   *Köttsoppa med rotsaker*

About 400 ml/¾ pt/1⅔ cups boiled
  beef, finely chopped or shredded (see
  Boiled Meat, page 30)
2 carrots
1 parsnip
about 100 g/3½ oz celeriac (celery-root)
1 leek or onion
1–1.25 l/1¾–2¼ pts/4¼–5¼ cups stock
salt
white or black pepper
finely chopped parsley

Peel carrots, parsnip, and celeriac. Rinse the leek or peel the onion. Cut all the vegetables into fine strips. Bring the stock to the boil and add the vegetables. Simmer gently until the vegetables are tender, about 10 min.
Add the meat and heat through. Season with salt and pepper. Sprinkle with parsley.

Variation: *Lamb Soup*   *Lammsoppa*
Substitute boiled lamb for the boiled beef and 500 g (1 lb) cabbage for the celeriac. Shred the cabbage. Proceed as above.

Variation: *Vegetable Soup with*
Dumpling   *Grönsakssoppa med klimp*
Follow the recipe for Meat and Vegetable Soup, but leave out the meat. Instead of meat stock you may use bouillon or vegetable broth.

Dumpling:
50 g/1¾ oz/scant ¼ cup butter
60 g/2 oz/scant ½ cup flour
300 ml/good ½ pt/1¼ cups milk
3–4 bitter almonds or 1 tsp almond
  extract
1 egg
¼ tsp salt
3 rounded tbs/scant ¼ cup finely chopped parsley

Melt the butter in a saucepan. Blend in the flour. Add the milk, little by little, while stirring. Keep on stirring till the mixture is smooth and rather thick. Simmer for about 5 min. Blanch, skin, and grate or grind the almonds. Beat the egg. Mix almonds and egg into the mixture. Season with salt. Turn the mixture into a mould, rinsed with water. Sprinkle with parsley.
Set aside to cool.
Turn out the dumpling and serve it with the soup.

Vegetable Soup with Dumpling, recipe page 13.

Pea Soup with Pork 4–6 servings *Ärtsoppa med lägg eller bog*

500 g/1 lb 2 oz dried yellow peas
1 small, lightly salted pork knuckle,
  0.75–1 kg/1 ⅔–2¼ lb or 400 g/scant
  lb lightly salted pork shoulder
1.75 l/3 pts/7½ cups water
1 onion
½–1 tsp thyme and/or marjoram

Soak the peas in plenty of cold water for about 12 hours. Add 1 tbs salt per litre (1¾ pts/4¼ cups) water.

Place the pork knuckle in a pot with the water and bring to the boil. Skim.

Peel and slice the onion. Add it to the meat. Cover and simmer on low heat for about 1 hour.

Drain the peas and add them to the soup. Cover and boil until the meat is tender and the peas are soft, a further 1–1½ hours. N.B. If pork shoulder is used, it should be put on at the same time as the peas, as it needs less cooking time than pork knuckle. Remove the meat. Cut it into slices or dice. Put it back into the soup or hand it separately.

Season the soup with thyme and/or marjoram and salt, if needed.

Serve with mustard.

Peas with pork, i.e. soup made with dried yellow peas, is a traditional Swedish family dish. The same recipe can be used for dried green peas.

Peas, which have not been soaked, will need to cook for 2–2½ hours.

Oxtail Soup 4 servings

1 oxtail, about 1 kg/2¼ lb, jointed
2 onions
1 carrot
1 parsnip
1 piece of celeriac, about 50 g/2 oz
butter
2 tsp salt
4 peppercorns, white or black
4 allspice berries
1 bay leaf
½–1 tsp thyme
2 tbs tomato purée
1.5 l/2⅔ pts/6⅓ cups water
2 tbs flour
1–2 tbs sherry or madeira (optional)

Trim off most of the fat from the oxtail. Peel the vegetables. Cut the onion into wedges and the root vegetables into pieces. Brown the meat and the vegetables in butter in a heavy-bottomed pot. Add salt, spices, tomato purée and water.

Cover and boil on low heat until the meat is tender, about 3 hours.

Remove the meat. Remove the bones and cut the meat into pieces.

Remove the vegetables.

Strain the stock and pour it back into the pot.

Mix the flour with 100 ml (3½ fl oz/scant ½ cup) water. Stir the thickening into the soup and boil for 3–5 min.

Return meat and vegetables to the pot. Correct seasoning and add optional sherry or madeira.

Fish Soup 4 servings

400 g/14 oz fresh or frozen fish fillets,
*   eg. cod, haddock, or plaice*
1 carrot
1 leek or onion
500 ml/18 fl oz/good 2 cups fish stock
1 packet frozen peas, about 250 g/½ lb
500 ml/18 fl oz/good 2 cups milk
3 tbs flour
3 tbs/scant ¼ cup finely chopped dill
½–1 tsp salt
¼ tsp white or black pepper

Rinse fresh fish fillets or partly thaw frozen ones. Peel the carrot and cut it into slices or dice. Rinse and shred the leek or peel and chop the onion. Place the vegetables in a saucepan with the fish stock. Boil for about 10 min.

Cut the fish fillets into pieces. Add fish and peas to the soup. Boil for a further 5 min.

Mix the flour with some of the milk and add the rest of the milk to the soup. Bring back to the boil and blend in the thickening.

Simmer on low heat for 3–5 min.

Add the dill and season with salt and pepper.

Kale Soup 4 servings

1 head of kale or 1 packet frozen kale,
*   about 375 g/13 oz*
1 l/1¾ pts/4¼ cups stock
2 tbs butter
3 tbs flour
100 ml/3½ fl oz/good ¾ cup cream
salt
white or black pepper

Rinse the fresh kale thoroughly. Remove any tough stalks. Bring the stock to the boil and add the kale. Boil for about 15 min. Drain the kale, but save the cooking liquid. Chop the kale finely. Melt the butter in a saucepan. Blend in the flour. Thin with stock and cream. Add the kale (if frozen kale is used, it can be added without thawing). Boil for some minutes. Season with salt and pepper.

Serve with boiled egg halves.

Nettle Soup—a spring speciality

Variation: *Spinach Soup*   *Spenatsoppa*
Substitute 375 g (6 oz) fresh spinach or 1 packet frozen spinach, about 375 g/13 oz for the kale.
Blanch the fresh spinach for 2–3 min. Chop it. Substitute milk for half of the stock. Proceed as described in the master recipe.

Variation: *Nettle Soup*   *Nässelsoppa*
Substitute 1½–2 l (2½–3½ pts/6½–8 cups) of young nettle shoots for the kale. Season the soup with a little chopped chives. Proceed as described in the master recipe.

Spring Vegetable Soup 4 servings

Ängamat

1 small cauliflower, about 200 g/7 oz
6 small carrots, about 175 g/6 oz
about 150 g/5 oz fresh sugar peas (snow peas)
about 60 g/2 oz fresh spinach
700 ml/1¼ pts/3 cups water
1½–2 tsp salt
1 tbs flour
500 ml/18 fl oz/good 2 cups milk
1 egg yolk
50 ml/1¾ fl oz/scant ¼ cup cream

Rinse the vegetables. Cut into strips or dice. Boil the vegetables in slightly salted water until barely tender, about 5 min. (Start with the vegetables, which require the longest cooking time.)

Mix the flour with 100 ml (3½ fl oz/scant ½ cup) of the milk. Blend this thickening into the soup. Boil for 3–5 min.

Add the rest of the milk and bring to the boil.

Beat the egg yolk and the cream together, and stir into the soup. The soup must not boil after this.

Spring Vegetable Soup, traditionally called Meadow Food, is a summer dish, but it can be made throughout the year with mixed frozen vegetables.

Cabbage Soup 4 servings

½ cabbage, about 750 g/1⅔ lb
1 l/1¾ pts/4¼ cups stock
4 allspice berries
6 white peppercorns
1 bay leaf
salt
soy sauce (optional)

Rinse the cabbage and shred it finely. Bring the stock to the boil with the spices. Add the cabbage. Cover and boil until the cabbage is tender, about 15 min. Season with salt. Add a few drops of optional soy sauce to improve the colour of the soup.
Serve with meatballs (see recipe below) or sausages.

Variation: *Browned Cabbage Soup*   *Brynt kålsoppa*
Fry the cabbage in butter in a heavy-bottomed pot until lightly browned. Add the stock and proceed according to the master recipe.

Variation: *Scanian Cabbage Soup*   *Skånsk kålsoppa*
Simmer 300 g/10 oz lightly salted pork shoulder or lean bacon (pork) for 1–1½ hours (cf. boiled meat, page 30). Clean and shred the cabbage as described above. Peel 2–3 carrots and 3–4 potatoes and slice them thinly. Boil the vegetables in the pork stock for about 15 min.
Dice the meat and add it to the soup. Sprinkle with chopped parsley.

Meatballs 4 servings

250 g/9 oz minced meat (ground beef)
1 egg
100 ml/3½ fl oz/scant ½ cup milk or cream
1½ tsp potato flour (potato starch)
½ tsp salt
¼ tsp white pepper
(500 ml/18 fl oz/good 2 cups stock)

Mix meat, egg, milk or cream, potato flour, and seasoning. Stir vigorously until the mixture is smooth. Form into small balls and put them on a board rinsed with water.
Poach the meatballs in the soup for 5–8 min. (They can also be poached in stock).

Broad Bean Soup 4 servings

2 kgs/4½ lb broad beans in their pods or 750 ml hulled broad beans (about 500 g/good lb)
2 carrots
1 l/1¾ pts/4¼ cups water
1 tsp salt
500 ml/18 fl oz/good 2 cups milk
3 tbs flour
1 egg yolk
100 ml/3½ fl oz/scant ½ cup cream
chopped parsley

Hull and rinse the beans. Peel and slice the carrots. Bring the water to the boil with the salt. Add beans and carrots. Cover and simmer until the vegetables are tender, about 40 min.
Mix the flour with some of the milk. Add the rest of the milk to the soup.
Bring back to the boil and blend in the thickening. Boil for a further 3–5 min.
Beat the egg yolk and the cream together and stir into the hot soup. The soup must not boil after this addition or it will curdle.
Sprinkle with parsley.

Potato Soup 4 servings

*8 medium-sized potatoes, about
    750 g/1⅔ lb
2–3 onions or leeks
butter
1 l/1¾ pts/4¼ cups stock
salt if needed
¼ tsp white or black pepper
3 tbs/scant ¼ cup finely chopped parsley
    and chives*

Peel and slice potatoes and onions. Rinse and shred the leeks. Soften the onions in butter in a saucepan. Add the stock and bring to the boil. Add the potatoes. Simmer until the potatoes are tender, about 15 min. Season with salt and pepper. Sprinkle with parsley and chives.

Variation: *Potato Soup with Spinach*   *Potatissoppa med spenat*
Use only six potatoes. Mix in 1 packet frozen chopped spinach, about 175 g (6 oz) when the potatoes are tender. Season with 1 tsp thyme. Omit the parsley and chives. Proceed as described above.

Variation: *Potato Soup with*   *Potatissoppa med brysselkål*
Brussels Sprouts
Use only 6 potatoes and omit the onions. Thaw 1 packet Brussels sprouts, about 250 g/8 oz. Slice the Brussels sprouts and add them to the soup when the potatoes have boiled for about 10 min. Boil for a further 5 min. Add 100 g (3½ oz) smoked ham or bacon, cut into strips. Season with ½ tsp tarragon. Omit parsley and chives. Proceed as described in the master recipe.

Fish

In the past fresh fish was, of course, only available along the coast and round the lakes. In the interior the fish was salted, dried, or fermented. Salted herring, dried cod, *lutfisk*, and fermented Baltic herring was eaten there. Today these dishes are considered delicacies.

Nowadays everyday fish dishes are mostly prepared from frozen fish, but the salted herring has kept an important place in Swedish cookery. It can be prepared in a large number of ways, simply fried, in gratins, even minced in patties. Salted herring for frying or pickling is available in tinned versions, which need no soaking.

Herring caught in the northern part of the Baltic is called *strömming* (Baltic herring). It is somewhat smaller (21–22 cm/9 in) than the herring caught in other waters, which may grow to 35–40 cm/14–16 in. Use small herrings in recipes calling for Baltic herring.

Fried Salt Herring with Onion Sauce 4 servings *Stekt saltsill med löksås*

2 large salted herrings or 4 salt herring fillets
3 tbs/scant ¼ cup coarse rye flour or breadcrumbs
2–3 tbs butter

Onion Sauce:
2 onions
1 tbs butter
2 tbs flour
400 ml/14 fl oz/1⅔ cups milk
½ tsp salt
¼ tsp white or black pepper

Clean and fillet the herrings. Skin the fillets and soak in cold water for about 15 hours. (Or use de-salted tinned frying herrings.)

Dry the fillets and dredge with rye flour or breadcrumbs. Heat the butter in a frying pan and fry the fillets on moderate heat until browned and crisp.

Sauce: Peel and chop the onions. Fry in butter in a saucepan until tender and lightly browned. Sprinkle on the flour and mix well. Thin with the milk while stirring. Simmer on low heat for about 5 min., stirring from time to time. Season with salt and pepper. Serve the herrings with the sauce and potatoes boiled in their jackets.

Herring au Gratin 4 servings *Sillpudding*

1 large salted herring or 2 salt herring fillets
10 medium-sized cold boiled potatoes
2 onions
butter
4 eggs
400 ml/14 fl oz/1⅔ cups milk
¼ tsp white or black pepper
chopped dill (optional)

Clean and fillet the herring. Skin the fillets and soak in cold water for 12 hours. (Or use de-salted, tinned frying herrings.) Cut the fillets into thin strips and slice the potatoes. Peel and slice the onions. Soften the onion in butter in a frying pan. Arrange potatoes, onions, and herring in alternate layers in a buttered ovenproof dish.

Beat eggs, milk, pepper, and optional dill together. Pour into the gratin dish.

Bake in a 225°C/435°F oven until the batter has set and the top is browned, about 30 min.

Serve with a raw vegetable salad and melted butter.

Steamed Salt Herring 4 servings

2 large salted herrings or 4 salt herring
    fillets
2 hard-boiled eggs
2 tbs butter
2 tbs each chopped dill and chopped
    chives

Clean, fillet, and skin the herrings. Soak the fillets in cold water for about 12 hours. (Or use de-salted tinned pickling herrings.) Peel and chop the eggs.

Butter an earthenware plate or dish, which fits on to your potato-saucepan. Place the herring fillets on the dish. Sprinkle with the chopped eggs, dill, and chives. Dot with butter. Place the dish over the boiling potatoes. Cover the dish and steam for 8–10 min. The potatoes must consequently have boiled a few minutes before the herrings are put on.

Serve the herrings with the freshly boiled potatoes.

Steamed Salt Herring—an old-fashioned Swedish Dish—is very easy to prepare.

Herring Patties with Currant Sauce 4 servings *Sillbullar med korintsås*

2 large salted herrings or 4 salt herring
   fillets
5 cold boiled potatoes
200 ml/7 fl oz/good ¾ cup cooked meat
100 ml/3½ fl oz/scant ½ cup milk
¼ tsp white pepper
3 tbs/scant ¼ cup breadcrumbs
butter

Sauce:
45 g/1½ oz/⅓ cup currants
400 ml/14 fl oz/1⅔ cups stock
1½ tbs maizena- or potato-flour + 50
   ml/1¾ oz/scant ¼ cup water
2 tbs vinegar
1 tbs treacle (molasses)
salt, soy sauce

Clean and fillet the herrings. Skin the fillets and soak in cold water for 15–20 hours. (Or use de-salted, tinned frying herrings.)

Put herrings, potatoes, and meat through the mincer. Blend in the milk and stir until the mixture is smooth and easy to shape. Form into flat, round patties and dredge with breadcrumbs. Fry the patties in butter on moderate heat until they are nicely browned and done, about 3 min. each side.

Sauce: Rinse the currants and simmer them in the stock until soft. Mix the maizena or potato flour with the water. Away from the heat blend the thickening into the sauce. If maizena is used, the sauce should be simmered for 2–3 min.; if potato flour is used, the sauce is brought back to the boil and taken off the heat.

Season with vinegar, treacle (molasses), salt, and soy sauce. Serve the herring patties with the sauce, boiled potatoes, and a raw vegetable salad.

Rolled Herring Sandwich 4 servings *Sillklämma*

2 rounds of soft tunnbröd
butter
4–6 cold boiled potatoes
2 fillets matjessill (sweet-pickled herring)
   or pickled salt herring
1 red onion

Halve the breads and spread them with the butter. Slice the potatoes and arrange them on the bread. Cut the herring fillets in pieces and put them on top of the potatoes.

Peel and chop the onion. Sprinkle over the herring.

Roll up the breads to form cones.

Herring and Potato Salad 4 servings *Sill- och potatissallad*

0.75–1 kg/1¾–2¼ lb cold boiled new
   potatoes
2 fillets of pickled salt herring
1 small red onion
3 tbs/scant ¼ cup finely chopped dill
200 ml/7 fl oz/good ¾ cup soured
   cream

Slice the potatoes, dice or shred the herring. Peel and chop the onion. Arrange the potatoes, herring, onion, and dill in alternate layers in a dish.

Fold the soured cream lightly into the salad.

Serve with crisp bread.

Caviar Herrings 4 servings *Kaviarströmming*

1 kg/2¼ lb Baltic herrings or
   600 g/1⅓ lb gutted herrings

Stuffing:
1 small tube of Swedish caviar, about
   100 g/3½ oz
1 bunch dill
100 ml/3½ fl oz/scant ½ cup cream
1 tsp salt
1 tbs breadcrumbs

Gut and rinse the herrings and remove the backbones. Spread the caviar on the inside of the herrings and roll them up. Arrange the rolled herrings in a buttered ovenproof dish. Chop the dill. Mix cream, dill, and salt. Pour it over the herrings. Sprinkle with breadcrumbs. Bake in a 225°C/435°F oven for about 20 min. Serve with boiled potatoes and a raw vegetable salad.

Fried Baltic Herrings

4 servings

Stekt strömming

1 kg/2¼ lb Baltic herrings
50 g/1¾ oz/scant ½ cup coarse rye flour
* or breadcrumbs*
1½ tsp salt
¼ tsp white or black pepper
2 tbs butter

Cut the herrings, but do not remove the backbones. Rinse under the water tap, drain, and dry.

Mix rye flour or breadcrumbs with salt and pepper. Coat the herrings with this mixture. Fry the herrings in butter on moderate heat until browned and done, 3–5 min. each side.

Serve with mashed potatoes (see page 47), a raw vegetable salad, and lingonberry jam (optional).

Red Herrings 4 servings

Kräftströmming

1 kg/2¼ lb Baltic herrings or
   600 g/1⅓ lb gutted herrings
1–1½ tsp salt
3–4 fresh heads of dill or 1 tbs dill seeds
3 tbs tomato purée
100 ml/3½ fl oz/scant ½ cup water
chopped dill

Gut and rinse the herrings. Remove the backbones. Sprinkle with salt.

Roll up the herrings with the fleshside outwards. Pack the rolls tightly in a buttered, wide, shallow pan.

Cut the heads of dill in pieces and sprinkle them or the dill seeds over the herrings. Mix tomato purée and water. Pour over the herrings.

Cover and simmer on low heat until the herrings are done, about 10 min.

Sprinkle with dill.

Serve with boiled potatoes. This dish may also be served cold.

Fish-balls 4 servings

Fiskbullar

400 g/14 oz fish-balls, tinned or frozen

Sauce:
1 tbs butter
2 tbs flour
200 ml/7 fl oz/good ¾ cup each milk
   and liquor from the fish-balls or fish
   stock
½ tsp salt

Heat tinned fish-balls in their liquor, frozen ones in fish stock.

Sauce: Melt the butter in a saucepan. Blend in the flour. Thin with the liquid while stirring. Simmer on low heat for 3–5 min. Add one of the seasonings.

Serve the fish-balls with the sauce, boiled potatoes, and green peas.

Seasoning:
- 3 tbs/scant ¼ cup each finely chopped parsley and chives
- 3 tbs/scant ¼ cup finely chopped dill, grated rind and juice of ½ lemon
- 2 tsp curry powder (cook the curry powder with the butter from the start)
- 2–3 tbs grated horseradish

Kabeljo (dried, salted cod) 4 servings

Kokt kabeljo

0.75–1 kg/1¾–2¼ lb dried salted cod
water
1–2 onions
parsley sprigs
75 g/scant 3 oz/⅓ cup butter
2 hard-boiled eggs
3 tbs/scant ¼ cup chopped parsley

Soak the cod in plenty of water for about 24 hours. Change the soaking water once.

Drain the fish and place in a saucepan.

Cover the fish with cold water. Bring to the boil.

Peel the onions and cut them in halves. Add onions and a few parsley sprigs to the fish. Cover and simmer on low heat until the fish is done, 25–30 min.

Melt the butter. Peel and chop the eggs. Mix eggs and parsley with the melted butter.

Take out the fish and place on a serving dish.

Serve with the egg and parsley butter and boiled potatoes.

Fried Baltic Herrings with Mashed Potatoes and Fried Herrings in Vinegar.

Fish Pudding   4 servings

135 g/scant 5 oz/²/₃ cup round-grained
  rice
300 ml/½ pt/1¼ cups water
½ tsp salt
600 ml/good pt/2½ cups milk
2 eggs
about 500 ml/18 fl oz/good 2 cups
  boiled fish (see recipe below)
½–1 tsp salt
¼ tsp white pepper
1 tbs breadcrumbs

To serve:
75 g/2²/₃ oz/⅓ cup butter

Boil the rice in salted water for about 15 min. Add milk and simmer on very low heat for another 30 min. Beat the eggs. Mix the eggs, the fish—cut into pieces—salt, and pepper into the rice.
Turn the mixture into a buttered ovenproof dish and sprinkle with breadcrumbs.
Bake in a 225°C/435°F oven for 40–45 min.
Serve with melted butter and boiled vegetables, for instance French beans.

Variation: *Pudding with Salted Cod*   *Kabeljopudding*
Substitute boiled, salted cod (see page 25) for the fish in the recipe above. Proceed as described above.

Caviar Gratin   4 servings

10 medium-sized potatoes
2 onions
300 ml/good ½pt/1¼ cups cream
100 g/3½ oz Swedish caviar
finely chopped dill

Peel the potatoes and cut them into matchstick lengths. Peel the onions and slice thinly. Mix caviar and cream. In a buttered ovenproof dish place alternate layers of potatoes and onions. Pour over the caviar-cream mixture. Cook in a 200°C/400°F oven until the top is browned and the potatoes are tender, 40–45 min. Sprinkle with dill.
Serve with a raw vegetable salad.

Cod with Egg- and Parsley-Sauce   4 servings   *Torsk med ägg- och persiljesås*

4 slices of cod, about 3 cm/1¼ in thick,
  cut across the fish or 600 g/1⅓ lb cod
  fillets
some parsley sprigs
½ leek
water
1 tsp salt per 500 ml/18 fl
  oz/good 2 cups water
5 white peppercorns

Sauce:
2 tbs butter
2 tbs flour
200 ml/7 fl oz/good ¾ cup each fish
  stock and milk
2 hard-boiled eggs
50 ml/3 rounded tbs finely chopped
  parsley
½–1 tsp salt
¼ tsp white pepper

Rinse the fish and drain. Cut the fillets into serving pieces. Rinse the parsley and the leek.
Place the fish in a wide, shallow saucepan. Measure the water and pour in enough to cover the fish. Add salt, peppercorns, parsley sprigs, and leek.
Bring to the boil, cover, and simmer on very low heat until the fish is white and firm, 8–10 min.

Sauce: Melt the butter in a saucepan. Blend in the flour and thin with the cooking liquid and the milk. Simmer on low heat, stirring, for 3–5 min. Peel and chop the eggs. Stir the eggs and the parsley into the sauce. Season with salt and pepper.
Remove the fish and place it on a serving dish. Serve with the sauce, boiled potatoes, and green peas.

Fish Gratin with Spinach   4 servings

Fiskgratäng med spenat

600 g/1⅓ lb fish fillets, eg. cod or plaice
1 tsp salt
¼ tsp white or black pepper
juice of ½ lemon
butter
1 packet frozen spinach leaves, about
*   250 g/8 oz*

Sauce:
2 tbs butter
2 tbs flour
150 ml/¼ pt/⅔ cup cooking liquid + fish
*   stock*
150 ml/¼ pt/⅔ cup cream
½ tsp salt
1 tsp chevril
1 tbs finely chopped parsley
100 ml/3½ fl oz/scant ½ cup grated
*   cheese, eg. of Cheddar type*

Sprinkle the fish with salt and pepper. Fold the fillets and place in a buttered ovenproof dish. Add the lemon juice. Cover the dish with aluminium foil.

Cook the fish in a 225°C/435°F oven for about 20 min.

Pour off and measure the cooking liquid. Add fish stock to make up 150 ml. Preheat the oven to 250°C/480°F. Thaw the spinach.

Sauce: Melt the butter in a saucepan. Blend in the flour. Thin with fish stock and cream while stirring. Simmer for 3–5 min. Add salt, chevril, and parsley.

Place the spinach around the fish fillets in the dish. Cover with the sauce. Sprinkle with grated cheese. Cook in a 250°C/480°F oven until nicely browned, about 15 min.

Serve with boiled, mashed, or riced potatoes, a tomato salad, or a green salad.

Burbot in Cream Sauce   4 servings

Stuvad lake

1–1.5 kg/2–3½ lb burbot
1 tbs salt
2 tbs butter
1 tbs flour
3 tbs unsweetened breadcrumbs
5 white peppercorns
5 allspice berries
1 bay leaf
1 small piece of mace
200 ml/7 fl oz/good ¾ cup water
150 ml/¼ pt/⅔ cup cream
1½–2 tbs lemon juice

Garnish:
parsley
lemon slices

Clean and skin the fish. Cut into pieces, about 4 cm/1½ in thick, across the backbone. Sprinkle with salt. Spread the butter in a wide, shallow saucepan. Place the fish in the pan, sprinkling it with flour, breadcrumbs, and spices. Add water and cream. Simmer on low heat until the fish is white, firm, and done, 15–20 min.

Season with lemon juice. Garnish with parsley and lemon slices. Serve straight from the pan with boiled potatoes.

Perch in Cream Sauce   4 servings

Stuvad abborre

1–1.25 kg/2¼–2¾ lb perch
1½ tsp salt
2 tbs butter
100 ml/3½ fl oz/scant ½ cup chopped
    dill or parsley
8 white peppercorns
2 tbs flour
200–250 ml/7–9 fl oz/¾–1 cup water
100 ml/3½ fl oz/scant ½ cup cream
1½–2 tbs lemon juice

Clean, scale, and rinse the perch, fillet and skin them if you wish. Sprinkle with salt.

Butter a wide, shallow saucepan. Arrange whole fish with their backs upwards, fold or roll up fillets. Sprinkle with dill or parsley and with coarsely ground pepper.

Mix the flour with a little of the water and pour this mixture, with the rest of the water, over the fish. Cover and poach on low heat for about 15 min. The cooking-time for fillets is approximately 8 min.

Shake the pan from time to time to prevent the fish from sticking to the bottom. Thin with the cream and season with lemon juice.

Serve straight from the pan with boiled potatoes.

Perch is a freshwater fish, but it is also found in the Baltic.

Grilled Whitebait 4 servings

1 kg/2¼ lb whitebait
1½ tbs salt
2 tbs cooking oil

Clean, rinse, and trim the fish. Place the fish in a bowl, sprinkle them with salt, and pour the oil over them. Marinate for about 30 min., turning the fish from time to time.
Grill the whitebait on a hot pan until they are nicely browned and done, about 4 min. each side. Whitebait can also be grilled on a rack over charcoal.
Serve at once with creamed potatoes or spinach, se page 52 or page 58.

Fried Mackerel 4 servings

2 mackerels, about 1 kg/2¼ lb
2–3 tbs breadcrumbs
1½–2 tsp salt
2 tbs butter

Clean, rinse, and fillet the mackerels. Carefully remove all the bones, but leave the skin on.
Coat the fillets with a mixture of breadcrumbs and salt.
Heat the butter in a frying pan. Fry the flesh-side of the fillets first, on low heat. Turn and fry the skin-side. Allow about 4–5 min. for each side.
Serve the fillets at once; with creamed spinach (see page 58) and boiled potatoes.

Meat

Meat has always been important in Swedish food. The everyday meat was salted, fatty pork. A pig could weigh up to 200 kg (440 lb) when it was slaughtered. Salted bacon was often dried to *spickefläsk*. Blood and entrails were utilized, among other things, together with fatty pork for sausage meat. The sausages were smoked, salted, or dried.

The beef was often of a poor quality, as the cows were skinny and allowed to grow too old before they were slaughtered. Also here most of the carcass was utilized, including the tripe and the udder. Much of the meat was salted. Boiled salted brisket of beef was a popular dish.

Mutton was part of the daily fare, whilst lamb and veal were reserved for festive occasions.

Nowadays the fresh Swedish meat is of good quality and the consumption of beef as well as pork has increased. Compared with other countries, however, the meat consumption in Sweden is still low.

Pork is, of course, still very important, and there are many different ways of preparing it, fresh or lightly salted. There are also many casserole-dishes where beef, lamb, or veal is cooked together with vegetables, especially winter vegetables like carrots, turnips, and cabbage.

Minced meat (beef, pork, veal, and lamb) is used a lot in Swedish everyday cooking. The Swedish meatballs are well known, but there are many varieties with interesting seasonings, for instance the Hamburger à la Lindström on page 43.

Reindeer (Am. caribou) meat used to be a regional speciality, but is now available frozen throughout Sweden. It may be found in delikatessen shops stocking Scandinavian food. You may use elk (Am. moose) or venison as a substitute.

Meat with Various Sauces 4 servings *Kokt kött med olika såser*

1 kg/2¼ lb bone-in meat, eg. brisket, top ribs, or shoulder of beef or veal; leg, shoulder, or ham of pork; breast, neck, or shoulder of lamb
water
2 tsp salt per liter/1¾ pts/4¼ cups water
2 carrots
1–2 onions
50 g/1¾ oz celeriac (celery-root)
1 parsnip (optional)
6 white peppercorns
6 allspice berries
1 bay leaf

Place the meat in a saucepan. Measure the water and pour in enough barely to cover the meat. Add salt and bring to the boil. Skim carefully.

Peel the vegetables and cut them into pieces. Add seasoning and vegetables.

Cover and simmer on low heat. Allow a cooking-time of 1½–2 hours for beef; 1¼–1½ hours for veal; 1–1½ hours for pork (up to 2 hours for pork shoulder); ¾–1½ for lamb. Pierce with a fork to test whether the meat is tender.

Remove the vegetables as soon as they are tender.

Sauce:
1 tbs butter
2½ tbs flour
500 ml / 18 oz / good 2 cups liquid (stock
+ optional milk)
1 egg yolk + 50 ml / 1¾ fl oz / scant ¼ cup
cream (optional)

Seasonings:
- *about 2 tbs grated horseradish*
- *1 tbs lemon juice*
  3 tbs chopped dill
- *1 tbs chrushed mustard seeds*
salt
white pepper

Sauce: Melt the butter in a saucepan and blend in the flour. Thin with stock and optional milk. Boil for 3–5 min. Add one of the seasonings. Blend the egg yolk and the cream together and stir into the hot sauce. The sauce must not boil after this addition, or it will curdle.
Carve the meat.
Serve with the sauce, boiled vegetables, and boiled potatoes.

Variation: *Boiled Salted Meat*
Proceed as for boiled meat, but choose for instance slightly salted brisket of beef, rolled ribs of beef, slightly salted ham, pork shoulder or knuckle, salted tongue of beef, veal, or pork. Allow about 250 g (9 oz) per serving of bone-in meat, about 125 g (4½ oz) of boneless salted meat. Omit the salt when boiling.
If the meat is very salty, it has to soak for a couple of hours before boiling. If it is lightly salted, it will only need rinsing.
Taste the stock after half the boiling-time. If it is too salty, pour it off, and pour in cold water. Bring back to the boil and simmer until the meat is tender.
Serve boiled salted meat with boiled root vegetables or mashed turnips (see page 62).

Salted meat is served with mashed turnips (see page 62) or mashed potatoes. (page 47).

Grilled Pork Knuckle 4 servings

1 lightly salted pork knuckle

Coating:
1 egg
3 tbs prepared mustard
breadcrumbs

Boil the pork knuckle as described for boiled salted meat, see page 31.
Remove the meat and skin it. Place the meat on a rack in a roasting pan.
Mix egg and mustard. Spread this mixture over the meat. Sprinkle with breadcrumbs. Brown in a 200°C/400°F oven for about 15 min. Serve with mashed potatoes or mashed turnips (see page 47 and page 62).

Chicken with Curry- or Lemon- Sauce 4–5 servings

1 boiling chicken, about
* 1.25 kg/2¾ lb*

To boil:
water
2 tsp salt per liter/1¾ pts/4¼ cups water
1 bay leaf
8–10 white peppercorns
1 small onion
some parsley sprigs

Thaw the chicken according to the directions. Place the chicken in a saucepan. Measure the water and pour in enough to cover the chicken. Add salt.
Bring to the boil and skim carefully. Add the spices, onion, and parsley. Simmer on low heat for 1–1½ hours. Test with a fork. Strain the stock and use some of it for the sauce. The surplus is excellent for making soup.
Carve the chicken and serve with potatoes or rice, curry- or lemon- sauce, and boiled broccoli or a raw vegetable salad.

Curry Sauce:
3 tsp curry powder
2 tbs butter
2 tbs flour
400 ml/14 fl oz/1⅔ cups chicken stock
50 ml/1¾ fl oz/scant ¼ cup cream
salt

Cook the curry in the butter in a saucepan. Blend in the flour and thin with the stock. Simmer on low heat for 3–5 min. Add the cream. Season with salt.

Lemon Sauce:
2 tbs butter
2 tbs flour
400 ml/14 fl oz/1⅔ cups chicken stock
salt
white or black pepper
2 tbs lemon juice + 1 tsp grated lemon
* rind*
1 egg yolk
100 ml/3½ fl oz/scant ½ cup cream

Melt the butter in a saucepan. Blend in the flour and thin with the stock.
Simmer for 3–5 min. Season with salt and pepper. Add lemon juice and rind. Mix egg yolk and cream. Away from the heat stir the egg mixture into the sauce. Do not let it boil, or it will curdle.

The chicken is here served with curry sauce.

Bouillon   2–3 l/3½–5¼ pts

2 kg/4½ lb beef with plenty of bones, eg.
 neck, shin, shoulder, or brisket
4 l/7 pts/good 4 quarts water
3 tsp salt
8–10 white peppercorns
1 carrot
1 onion or leek
1 small piece of celeriac (celery-root) or
 1 stalk of celery, about 50 g/1¾ oz
some parsley sprigs

Rinse the meat under the cold water tap. Cut it up in smaller pieces. The bones should be cracked or cut. Place meat and bones in a soup pot. Add cold water and salt. Bring to the boil and skim carefully. Add the peppercorns. Cover and simmer on low heat for about 2 hours. Peel the vegetables and cut them into pieces. Add the vegetables to the pot. Simmer for another 2–4 hours.

Strain the stock. Cool as quickly as possible. Refrigerate. Do not remove the congealed fat until you are ready to use the stock. It keeps the air out and helps to preserve the stock. The bouillon may be frozen for future use.

Clarified Bouillon:
Beat 2 egg whites lightly in a saucepan. Pour in the cold stock (without fat and sediment). Bring to the boil slowly, stirring slowly and continously. Let the stock simmer for 5 min. Remove the saucepan from the heat and let stand covered for 10–15 min.
Strain the stock through a cheesecloth. Chill the clarified stock quickly.

Brown Bouillon:
Follow the master recipe, but brown the meat before boiling. If you have a lot of meat you may brown it in a roasting pan in a 250°C/480°F oven for about 30 min.

Swedish Beef Stew   4 servings

400–500 g/about 1 lb boneless beef, eg.
 shoulder
2 onions
2 tbs butter
2 tbs flour
1½ tsp salt
10–12 allspice berries
3 bay leaves
about 400 ml/¾ pt/1⅔ cups water

Cut the meat into 3 cm (1¼ in) cubes. Peel and slice the onions. Heat the butter in a frying pan and brown the meat, a little at a time, and then the onions. Transfer to a saucepan. Sprinkle with the flour, add salt, allspice berries, and bay leaves. Deglaze the frying pan with some of the water and pour this gravy over the meat.

Cover and let the stew simmer on low heat for 1¼–1½ hours. Stir from time to time and add more water if needed. Serve with boiled potatoes, pickled beetroots, and a raw vegetable salad.

Variation: *Beef Stew with Anchovies*   *Köttgryta med ansjovis*
Follow the master recipe, but use only 1 tsp salt and 5 allspice berries.
Add 4–5 Swedish anchovy fillets (or anchovies in oil) and 4 white peppercorns. Substitute cream for 100–150 ml (3½–5½ fl oz/scant ½–¾ cup) of the water. The cream will give the stew a mild flavour.
Serve with boiled potatoes and a raw vegetable salad.

Chantarelles and juniper berries give the stew a delicious flavour.

Variation: *Beef Stew with Vegetables*   Köttgryta med grönsaker
Follow the master recipe, but substitute 8–10 white pepper-corns for the allspice berries. About 30 min. before the meat is done, add appr. 300 g/10 oz turnips, 2 carrots, 1 parsnip, and 50 g/1¾ oz celeriac (celery-root) or 1 stalk of celery, all peeled and cut into strips or pieces. Let the stew simmer until the meat is tender and the vegetables feel soft when pierced with a fork. Sprinkle with chopped parsley. Serve with boiled potatoes.
You may also prepare this stew without browning the meat. In that case, place the meat directly in a saucepan, pour on water and add salt. Bring to the boil and skim. Add the spices, cover, and simmer on low heat.

Variation: *Beef Stew with Chanterelles*   Köttgryta med kantareller
Follow the master recipe, but substitute 5 white pepper-corns and 10 lightly crushed Juniper berries for the allspice berries. Fry 200 g/7 oz chanterelles (fresh, tinned, or frozen) in butter. Add them to the stew about 30 min. before the meat is tender.
Serve with boiled potatoes and French beans.

Veal Casserole 4 servings

0.75–1 kg/1¾–2¼ lb bone-in veal, eg.
from the shoulder
2 onions
butter
2 tbs flour
1½ tsp salt
¼ tsp white or black pepper
1 tsp crumbled rosemary
2 tbs tomato purée
200 ml/7 fl oz/good ¾ cup water
100 ml/3½ fl oz/scant ½ cup cream

Cut the meat away from the bones and cut it into strips. Keep the bones. Peel and chop the onions. Heat the butter in a frying pan and brown the meat, a little at a time. Transfer to a saucepan. Brown the onions and then the bones. Add to the saucepan. Sprinkle with flour. Add salt, spices, and tomato purée. Deglaze the frying pan with the water and add to the stew. Cover and simmer on low heat for about 15 min. Add the cream, and simmer for another 10 min., until the meat feels tender when pierced with a fork. Check the seasoning and add more salt and pepper if needed. Serve with boiled potatoes and a salad.

Variation: *Veal Casserole with Baby Onions*
and Mushrooms   *Kalvgryta med smålök och champinjoner*
Substitute 10–12 baby onions and 200 g/7 oz fresh or tinned mushrooms for the chopped onions. Brown baby onions and mushrooms and let them simmer with the stew. If you wish, use only 1 tbs tomato purée.

Lamb Stew 4 servings

0.75–1 kg/1¾–2¼ lb bone-in lamb, eg.
from the shoulder or neck
10–12 baby onions
200 g/7 oz chanterelles, fresh or tinned
butter
1–1½ tsp salt
¼ tsp white or black pepper
200 ml/7 fl oz/good ¾ cup water or
stock
50 ml/3 rounded tbs finely chopped
parsley

Cut the meat into 3 cm (1¼ in) pieces. Keep the bones and let them simmer with the stew.
Peel the baby onions. This is easy, if you rinse them in hot water first. Trim and rinse the fresh mushrooms, drain the tinned ones.
Heat the butter in a frying pan and brown the meat, a little at a time, and transfer to a stewpan. Add salt (a little less it you use stock) and pepper. Add water or stock.
Simmer on low heat until the meat is tender, 30–40 min.
Meanwhile, brown the baby onions and the chanterelles in butter in the frying pan.
Add to the stewpan when about 5 min. of the cooking-time is left. Sprinkle with parsley.
Serve with boiled potatoes and a salad.

Lamb Stew with Cabbage 4 servings

0.75–1 kg/1¾–2¼ lb sliced, bone-in
lamb, eg. from the neck or shoulder
½ cabbage, about 0.75 kg/1¾ lb
butter
200–300 ml/⅓–½ pt/¾–1¼ cups water
2 tsp salt
10 white peppercorns
1 bay leaf
finely chopped parsley

Rinse and shred the cabbage. Brown the meat in butter in a frying pan. Arrange meat and cabbage in alternate layers in a stewpan. Deglaze the frying pan with a little water and pour the pan juices into the stewpan. Add seasoning. Cover and simmer on low heat for 30–40 min. Add more water if needed. Sprinkle with parsley.
Serve with boiled potatoes.

Beefsteak à la Nelson (Seafarer's Beef) 4 servings *Sjömansbiff*

500 g/1 lb 2 oz boneless beef, eg. rump, top side, eyeround, bottomround or tenderized shoulder, cut into slices
3 large onions
butter
2–3 tsp salt
½ tsp white or black pepper
10–12 medium-sized potatoes, about 1 kg/2¼ lb
400–500 ml/14–18 fl oz/1¾–good 2 cups water, stock, and light lager beer (optional)

Peel and slice the onions. Heat the butter in a frying pan and brown the onions on low heat. Remove the onions and brown the meat, a little at a time, on moderately high heat. Sprinkle with a little salt and pepper. Be careful with the salt if you are using stock.

Peel and slice the potatoes.

Arrange potatoes, onions, and meat in alternate layers in a wide saucepan or casserole. The bottom and top layers should be potatoes. Season with salt and pepper between the layers. Deglaze the frying pan with water, stock, and optional lager beer. Add the pan juices to the casserole. Cover and simmer on low heat until the potatoes are soft and the meat tender, about 45 min.

Serve straight from the casserole with a salad.

Reindeer (Caribou) Stew 4 servings *Renragu*

500 g/1 lb 2 oz boneless reindeer meat, eg. from saddle or roast. Elk (Am. moose) or venison may be substituted for reindeer
1 small piece of celeriac (celery-root) or 1 stalk of celery, about 50 g/1 ¾ oz
1–2 leeks or onions
butter
2 tbs flour
1–1½ tsp salt
¼ tsp white or black pepper
1 tsp thyme
about 400 ml/14 fl oz/1 ⅔ cups stock
50 ml/1 ¾ fl oz/scant ¼ cup cream

Cut the meat into 2 cm (¾ in) cubes. Peel and dice the celeriac. Rinse and slice the leeks, or peel and chop the onions.

Heat the butter in a frying pan and brown the meat, a little at a time. Transfer to a saucepan. Brown the onions. Add the celeriac and let it soften for a minute or two. Transfer to the saucepan. Sprinkle with flour. Season with salt, pepper, and thyme. Pour in the stock.

Cover and simmer until the meat is tender, 30–40 min. Thin with cream towards the end of the cooking-time.

Serve with boiled potatoes or rice, French beans, or a salad.

Mustard-flavoured Reindeer Meat 4 servings *Renskav med senapssmak*

2 packets frozen renskav, appr. 240 g/8 oz each
1 large onion
butter
3 tbs prepared mustard
150 ml/¼ pt/⅔ cup cream
200 ml/7 fl oz/good ¾ cup stock
1–1½ tsp salt
¼ tsp white or black pepper

Renskav is very thinly sliced meat of reindeer (Am. caribou). It is normally marketed frozen. If reindeer meat is obtainable, cut it into very thin slices, 1 mm (less than ¹⁄₁₆ in). This is easiest done when the meat is partly frozen. Elk (Am. moose) or venison may be used as substitute.

Partly thaw the meat. Peel and chop the onions. Melt the butter in a frying pan and brown the meat and onion, a little at a time, separating the meat slices with a fork. Transfer to a saucepan. Mix mustard and cream. Stir in the cream mixture and the stock. Cover and simmer on low heat for about 5 min. Season with salt and pepper.

Serve with boiled potatoes or rice and salad.

Fried Pork Chops 4 servings

4 pork chops, about 600 g/1 1/3 lb
1 tbs butter
1–1 1/2 tsp salt
1/4 tsp white or black pepper

Serving Suggestions:
• *with chanterelles and cream*
200 g/7 oz chanterelles (fresh or tinned)
1/2 tbs butter
200 ml/7 fl oz/good 3/4 cup whipping
  cream
salt and pepper
soy sauce (optional)

• *with cheese:*
4 slices cheese, about 100 g/3 1/2 oz, a
  well-ripened cheese of Emmental or
  Cheddar type
1 tsp paprika

• *with mushrooms:*
1 leek
200 g/7 oz mushrooms (fresh or tinned)
1 tbs butter
50ml/3 rounded tbs finely chopped
  parsley

• *with sauce:*
100 ml/3 1/2 fl oz/scant 1/2 cup stock
1 1/2 tbs flour + 50 ml/1 3/4 fl oz/scant
  1/4 cup cold water
150 ml/1/4 pt/2/3 cup cream
salt and pepper
soy sauce (optional)

Heat the butter in a frying pan and fry the pork chops on a moderately high heat, 3–4 min. each side. Season with salt and pepper.

Trim and rinse fresh mushrooms, drain tinned ones. Fry the chanterelles in butter in a frying pan. Fry the pork chops as described above. Place the mushrooms on top of the pork chops in the pan. Pour in the cream. Simmer uncovered for a couple of minutes.
Season with salt, pepper, and optional soy sauce.
Serve with boiled potatoes and a salad.

Fry the pork chops as described above. After turning the chops in the pan, cover each with a slice of cheese. Cover the pan and finish cooking, letting the cheese melt and coat the meat.
Sprinkle with paprika.
Serve with boiled or riced potatoes (see page 54) and for instance a salad.

Rinse the leek and shred it finely. Trim and rinse fresh mushrooms, drain tinned ones.
Heat the butter in a frying pan. Soften the leek in the butter. Add the mushrooms and cook until all the liquid has evaporated and the leek and mushrooms are lightly browned. Blend in the parsley.
Fry the pork chops as described above. Garnish with the mushrooms.
Serve with boiled potatoes or panfried potatoes (see page 54) and a salad.

Fry the pork chops as described above. Add the stock. Cover the pan and let the pork chops cook for about 10 min. Remove the pork chops to a side dish and keep hot.
Mix the flour and the water. Stir this thickening into the pan juices. Add the cream and let the sauce simmer on low heat for 3–5 min. Season with salt, pepper, and optional soy sauce.
Serve the pork chops with the sauce, boiled potatoes, and boiled vegetables.

Fried Bacon, Swedish Style   4 servings   *Stekt fläsk*

400 g / 14 oz lightly salted, streaky bacon (salt pork), sliced rather thickly, about 5 mm / ¼ in

Put the bacon, a few slices at a time, in a cold frying pan. Fry the bacon on both sides in its own fat. Drain on paper towels.

Serving Suggestions:
● *Onion Sauce:*   *Löksås*
2 onions
1 tbs butter
2 tbs flour
400 ml / 14 fl oz / 1 ⅔ cups milk
½ tsp salt
¼ tsp white or black pepper

Peel and chop the onions. Heat the butter in a frying pan and cook the onions until soft. Sprinkle with flour and mix. Stir in the milk. Simmer on low heat for about 5 min. Season with salt and pepper.
Serve the bacon with the sauce and boiled potatoes in their jackets.

● *Brown Beans:*   *Bruna bönor*
see recipe on page 62

● *Black Bread with*   *Paltbröd och vit sås*
White Sauce:

Paltbröd was originally a kind of dumpling made with blood and barley flour and poached in water. Nowadays the name is used for a black round bread, seasoned with treacle (molasses) and spices. This bread is dried and then boiled in salted water.

1–2 rounds dried black bread
water
½ tbs salt per litre / 1 ¾ pts / 4 ¼ cups water

Break the black bread in pieces. Place them in a saucepan. Measure the water and pour in enough to cover the bread. Add salt. Cover and simmer on low heat until soft, 10–15 min.
Meanwhile prepare the sauce: Melt the butter in a saucepan. Blend in the flour. Thin with the milk. Simmer on low heat for 3–5 min. Season with salt and pepper. Take out the black bread with a slotted spoon and drain.
Serve the bacon with the black bread and the sauce.

● *Bacon with Apples:*   *Äppelfläsk*
2 onions
2–3 apples
¼ tsp white or black pepper
2–3 cloves (optional)

Peel and slice the onions. Peel, core, and slice the apples. Fry the onions and the apples in some of the bacon fat until lightly browned and soft. Arrange the bacon, the onions, and the apples in alternate layers in the frying pan and let all heat through. Season with pepper and cloves.
Serve with potatoes boiled in their jackets.

Home-made Black Pudding 2–2.5 kg/4½–5½ lb *Hemlagad blodpudding*

1 l/1¾ pts/4¼ cups pig's or calf's blood
800 ml/scant 1½ pts/3⅓ cups milk
450 g/1 lb/3¾ cups rye flour
1 small onion, red or yellow
50 g/1¾ oz/scant ¼ cup butter
100 g/3½ oz fresh pork fat (optional)
100 ml/3½ fl oz/scant ½ cup treacle
1½ tbs salt
1 tsp white pepper
½ tsp allspice
½ tsp ground cloves
1 tsp ground ginger
1 tsp marjoram

Thaw the blood, if it is frozen. Strain it. Mix blood, milk, and rye flour.

Peel and finely chop the onion. Soften it in the butter. Use less butter if pork fat is used as well. Dice the pork fat finely. Add onion and butter, optional pork fat, treacle (molasses), salt, and spices to the blood mixture.

Fry a spoonful of the mixture in butter in a frying pan to check the seasoning, and correct if needed.

Pour the mixture into two well-greased 1.5 l/3 pts rectangular moulds. Cover the moulds with aluminium foil. Place them in a tin containing enough warm water to come halfway up the outside of the moulds.

Place the tin in a 200°C/400°F oven and bake until the mixture has set, 1.5–2 hours.

Let the puddings cool a little before unmoulding. Black pudding may be served freshly-made or fried in slices, with lingonberry jam and a raw vegetable salad. It may also be frozen.

Black Pancakes 4 servings *Blodplättar*

500 ml/18 fl oz/good 2 cups pig's or
  calf's blood
400 ml/14 fl oz/1⅔ cups milk
1½ tsp salt
¼ tsp white or black pepper
125 g/4½ oz/good cup rye flour

Thaw the blood, if it is frozen. Strain it. Mix blood, milk, salt, and pepper. Beat in the rye flour. Fry the mixture in a frying pan or a crêpe pan, as thin pancakes or as small, blini-sized pancakes—*plättar*.

Serve at once with lingonberry jam.

Liver Pudding 4 servings *Korvkaka*

140 g/5 oz/good ¾ cup pearl barley
700 ml/1¾ pts/3 cups water
500 ml/18 fl oz/good 2 cups milk
300 g/10 oz pig's liver
100 g/3½ oz fresh belly pork
1 onion
2 tsp salt
¼ tsp white or black pepper
¼ tsp allspice
½ tsp ground ginger or marjoram
  (optional)
1 tbs treacle (molasses)

Put the pearl barley in a saucepan with the water. Cover and boil on low heat for 30 min. Add the milk and continue boiling for another 30 min, stirring from time to time. Rinse and drain the liver. Put liver, pork, and onion through the mincer.

Blend in the barley, salt, spices, and treacle. Fry a spoonful of the mixture to check the seasoning, and correct if needed. Pour the mixture into a greased ovenproof dish.

Bake in a 200°C/400°F oven, until browned and done, 40–50 min.

Serve with lingonberry jam and a raw vegetable salad.

Hash 4 servings

400 g/14 oz beef or pork, eg. from the shoulder, mixed with heart and/or liver (optional)
water
2 tsp salt per litre/1¾ pts/4¼ cups water
2 onions
140 g/5 oz/good ¾ cup pearl barley
800 ml/scant 1½ pts/3⅓ cups stock
½–1 tsp salt
¼ tsp white or black pepper
¼ tsp allspice
1 tsp marjoram

Boil meat, heart, and/or liver in lightly salted water until tender (see Boiled Meat, page 30). Add the peeled onions towards the end of the cooking-time.

Remove the meat and strain the stock. Boil the pearl barley in the stock for about 30 min. Put meat and onions through the mincer.

Mix the meat with the barley, and heat through. Moisten with stock if the mixture appears dry. Season with salt and spices. Serve with boiled potatoes and pickled beetroots.

Variation: *Hash with Fried Apples and Onions* *Pölsa med steka äppelskivor och lök*
Peel 2 onions and 2 tart apples. Core the apples. Slice onions and apples. Fry in butter until soft. Heat the hash with a little stock in a saucepan. Serve with onions and apples.

Variation: *Hash with Beetroot Salad*, see page 146
Heat the hash with a little stock in a saucepan. Serve with the salad.

Liver Ragoût 4 servings

500 g/1 lb 2 oz calf's liver
2 onions
butter
1 tbs flour
1 tsp salt
¼ tsp white or black pepper
1 tsp marjoram
100 ml/3½ fl oz/scant ½ cup stock
150 ml/¼ pt/⅔ cup cream

Cut the liver into strips or dice. Peel and chop the onions. Heat the butter in a frying pan and brown liver and onions. Sprinkle with flour. Season with salt and spices. Add the stock and the cream.
Cover and simmer on low heat for 5 min.
Correct seasoning.
Serve with boiled potatoes and a raw vegetable salad.

Variation: *Liver Casserole with Mushrooms* *Levergryta med svamp*

Follow the recipe above, but use only 1 onion and use 1 can of sliced mushrooms, appr. 200 g/7 oz.
Brown the drained mushrooms with the liver and onions. Substitute the mushroom liquor for the stock.

Variation: *Liver Casserole with Vegetables* *Levergryta med grönsaker*

Follow the master recipe, but substitute rinsed and shredded leeks for the onions. Add appr. 250 g/8 oz mixed frozen vegetables and simmer for 5 min. as above.

Higgler's Pot 4 servings

2 pig's kidneys, appr. 300 g/10 oz
300 g/10 oz boneless pork, eg. from the
*   shoulder*
2 onions
8–10 medium-sized potatoes, appr.
*   750 g/1⅔ lb*
2 tbs butter
2–3 tsp salt
½ tsp white or black pepper
1 bottle dark ale, 33 cl

Rinse the kidneys and blanch them, i.e. put them in cold, salted water (2 tsp salt per litre/1¾ pts/4¼ cups water). Bring to the boil and drain.

Slice the kidneys and the pork. Peel and slice the onions. Heat the butter in a frying pan and brown, separately, kidneys, pork, and onions.

Peel and slice the potatoes.

Arrange the ingredients in alternate layers in a saucepan. Season between the layers.

Add the ale. Cover and simmer on low heat until tender, about 25 min.

Serve with a salad.

Liver Patties 4 servings

400 g/14 oz calf's liver
6 medium-sized potatoes, about
*   500 g/1 lb 2 oz*
1 onion
50 g/1¾ oz smoked bacon
1½ tsp salt
¼ tsp white or black pepper
¼ tsp marjoram or thyme (optional)
butter
150 ml/¼ pt/⅔ cup each stock and
*   cream*
salt and pepper (optional)

Cut the liver into pieces convenient for mincing. Peel the potatoes and onion and cut them into pieces. Put the liver, bacon, potatoes, and onion through the mincer. Season the mixture with salt and spices.

Heat the butter in a frying pan. Put in spoonfuls of the mixture and fry until browned and done, 2–3 min. each side. Remove to a serving dish and keep hot.

When all the patties are cooked, pour the stock and cream into the pan. Boil down for a couple of minutes. Check seasoning and add salt and pepper if needed. Serve the liver patties with the gravy, boiled potatoes, lingonberry jam, and a raw vegetable salad.

Lamb Patties 4 servings

400 g/14 oz minced lamb
2 boiled potatoes
1 onion
butter
½ tsp ground allspice
½ tsp ground mustard seeds
1 tsp salt
300–400 ml/½–⅔ pt/1¼–1⅔ cups milk

Mash the potatoes. Peel and chop the onion. Soften the onion in a little butter.

Mix the minced lamb with potatoes, onion, and spices. The mixture should be well seasoned. Add milk until the consistency is soft.

Heat a little butter in a frying pan. When the butter is brown, put in spoonfuls of the mixture. Fry until browned and done, 2–3 min. each side.

Serve with boiled potatoes, lingonberry jam, and a raw vegetable salad.

Forcemeat—Master Recipe 4 servings

Köttfärs – grundrecept

*400 g/14 oz minced meat, eg. beef, beef
   and pork, or veal and pork
40 g/1½ oz/⅓ cup breadcrumbs or
   2 medium-sized cold, boiled potatoes
175–200 ml/6–7 fl oz/about ¾ cup milk
1–1½ tsp salt
¼ tsp white or black pepper
2 tbs chopped and lightly browned
   onion or 1 tbs grated raw onion*

Soak the breadcrumbs in the milk for about 10 min. or mash the potatoes. Mix the meat with the soaked breadcrumbs or the mashed potatoes and the milk (use less milk with potatoes), salt, pepper, and onion. Blend the mixture thoroughly.

Meatballs with Sauce
Köttbullar med sås

Using your hands, dipped in cold water, or two spoons, form the mixture into small meatballs of uniform size. Place them on a carving board, rinsed with cold water. Brown the meatballs, a few at a time, in a little butter in a frying pan. Shake the pan so that they brown evenly. When browned, transfer the meatballs to a saucepan. Deglaze the frying pan with 200 ml/7 fl oz/good ¾ cup stock and pour the gravy into the saucepan. Simmer until the meatballs are done, 8–10 min. Strain the gravy into a saucepan and add enough water or stock to make up 300 ml/½ pt/1¼ cup. Mix 1½ tbs flour with 50 ml/1¾ fl oz/scant ¼ cup cold water.
Beat this thickening into the boiling gravy. Simmer on low heat, 3–5 min. Add 50–100 ml/1¾–3½ fl oz/¼–½ cup cream (optional). Season with salt and pepper.
Serve with the sauce, boiled potatoes, and a salad.

Hamburgers with Onions
Pannbiff med lök

Form the forcemeat into flat, round patties, and place them on a carving board, rinsed with cold water. With a knife, cut a check pattern on the patties (optional). Peel and slice 3–4 onions. Brown the onions in butter in a frying pan. Transfer to a saucepan and add 50 ml/1¾ fl oz/scant ¼ cup water. Season with salt and pepper. Cover and cook on low heat. Remove the onions. Fry the hamburgers, a few at a time, in the frying pan, 4–5 min each side. Deglaze the pan with a little stock.
Serve with the gravy, the onions, boiled potatoes, and a raw vegetable sallad.

Hamburgers à la Lindström
Biff à la Lindström

Mix the forcemeat with 3 tbs finely chopped pickled cucumbers, 3 tbs finely chopped pickled beetroots, and 1 tbs capers. Form into flat patties. Fry as described above, but omit the onions.

Prune Birds
Plommonjärpar

Add 100 g (3½ oz) chopped prunes to the forcemeat made from pork. Form into cylinders, about 7 cm (3 in) long. Instead of mixing chopped prunes into the forcemeat, you may stuff each roll with ½ prune. Heat a little butter in a frying pan and brown the prune birds, a few at a time. Transfer to a saucepan. Deglaze the frying pan with 200 ml (7 fl oz/good ¾ cup) stock and pour the gravy into the saucepan. Simmer until the prune birds are done, about 10 min. Remove to a serving dish, and keep hot. Thin the gravy with stock to make up 300 ml (½ pt/1¼ cups). Make the sauce as described for meatballs. Serve the prune birds with the sauce, boiled potatoes, apple purée, and a salad or boiled vegetables.

Stuffed Cabbage Leaves   4 servings   *Kåldomar*

1 cabbage, about 1 kg/2¼ lb
water, 2 tsp salt per litre/1¾ pts/4¼ cups water

Stuffing:
70 g/2½ oz/⅓ cup round-grained rice
200 ml/7 fl oz/good ¾ cup water
300 g/10 oz minced meat
1–1½ tsp salt
¼ tsp white or black pepper
100–150 ml/3½–5½ fl oz/½–⅔ cup milk

butter
300 ml/½ pt/1¼ cups water or stock

Sauce:
400 ml/14 fl oz/1⅔ cups stock
2 tbs flour + 50 ml/1¾ fl oz/scant ¼ cup water

Cut out the lower part of the cabbage stem.
Bring water and salt to the boil in a big saucepan. Drop in the whole cabbage and boil for 8–10 min. Peel off the leaves one by one, remove, and drain carefully.
Boil the rice with the water for about 20 min. Set aside to cool. Blend the minced meat with rice, salt, pepper, and milk to a fairly soft mixture.
Place 2 tbs stuffing on each cabbage leaf. Roll up into sausage-shaped packages and secure with toothpicks.
Heat a little butter in a frying pan and brown the roulades. Transfer to a saucepan. Add water or stock. Cover and cook on low heat until the cabbage is soft and the stuffing done, 30–40 min.
Take out the cabbage roulades and remove the toothpicks.
Mix flour and water. Beat into the gravy. Simmer for 3–5 min. Correct seasoning.
Serve with the sauce, boiled potatoes, and lingonberry jam.

Cabbage Pudding   4 servings   *Kålpudding*

½ cabbage, 500–750 g/1–1½ lb
butter

Forcemeat:
300 g/10 oz minced meat
2 medium-sized cold boiled potatoes
1–1½ tsp salt
¼ tsp white or black pepper
300 ml/10 fl oz/1¼ cups milk

Rinse the cabbage and cut it into pieces. Brown it in butter in a frying pan.
Mash the potatoes. Mix the minced meat, potatoes, salt, and pepper. Thin with milk until the mixture is soft.
Arrange the cabbage and the forcemeat in alternate layers in a buttered ovenproof dish. The bottom and top layers should be cabbage.
Bake in a 200°C/400°F oven for 45–60 min. Add a little water, if the cabbage seems too dry.
Serve with boiled potatoes and lingonberry jam.

Stuffed Cabbage Leaves.

Falu Sausage Casserole 4 servings

400 g/14 oz Falu sausage (As a substitute Large sausages of Frankfurter or Strasbourg type, hot dogs or knockwurst can be used)
1 cabbage wedge, about 400 g/14 oz
1 apple
1 onion
200 ml/7 fl oz/good ¾ cup stock
1 tsp cumin
6–8 white peppercorns
salt and pepper (optional)
50 ml/3 rounded tbs chopped parsley

Falukorv is a lightly smoked and boiled sausage, made from beef and pork. It was originally a regional speciality (from Falun in Dalarna), but has now become the most popular sausage in Sweden.
Rinse and shred the cabbage. Peel and core the apple, and cut it into wedges. Peel and slice the onion. Place cabbage, apple, and onion in a saucepan. Add stock and spices. Cover and simmer on low heat until the cabbage is barely tender, about 15 min. Skin and slice the sausage. Put the sausage slices in the saucepan and cook for 5 min. more. Correct seasoning. Sprinkle with parsley. Serve with boiled potatoes.

Variation: *Pork Sausage with
Cumin Cabbage*   *Fläskkorv med kumminkål*

Boil 2–3 peeled and thinly sliced carrots with the cabbage. Skin a boiled pork sausage (appr. 300 g/10 oz). Slice the sausage and add to the cabbage. Proceed as described in the master recipe.

Sausage Casserole 4 servings

400 g/14 oz Falu sausage
6 medium-sized potatoes
½ turnip, about 500 g/1 lb 2 oz
3–4 carrots, about 250 g/9 oz
1 piece of celeriac, about 50 g/1¾ oz
400 ml/14 fl oz/1⅔ cups stock
salt and pepper to taste
100 ml/3½ fl oz/scant ½ cup chopped parsley

Peel the vegetables and cut them into thin pieces or strips. Place in a saucepan. Pour in the stock. Simmer the vegetables on low heat until barely tender, about 15 min. Skin the sausage and cut it into thin slices or strips. Add the sausage to the vegetables and heat through. Correct seasoning.
Sprinkle with parsley.

Fried *Isterband*

4 isterband, about 500 g/1 lb 2 oz

Serving Suggestions:
Potatoes in White Sauce, see page 52
Stewed Cabbage, see page 58
Beetroot Salad, see page 146

Isterband is a genuine Swedish sausage, which can be bought smoked or unsmoked (see recipe on page 150). *Isterband* have a fresh, slightly tart flavour. They may be fried, grilled, or roasted.
Fry the sausages in a frying pan or roast them in the oven.
In the frying pan: Put the *isterband*, whole, and without any extra fat, in a cold frying pan. Fry on moderate heat until browned and done, 5–8 min.
In the oven: Make a few cuts in the surface of the sausages. Place on a rack in a roasting tin. Cook in a 225°C/435°F oven until browned and done, about 10 min.
Serve with one of the suggested accompaniments.

Potatoes

Potatoes have been very important in the Swedish diet. During periods of food shortage, they have certainly saved many from undernourishment. It was impossible to imagine a day without potatoes. They were eaten boiled or fried, in a variety of dishes.

Boiled potatoes were used for dumplings, they could be used in sausages, and in various kinds of bread. Raw potatoes were grated and used for porridge and gruel, in sausages and meat dishes, and for potato pancakes.

Although the consumption of processed potatoes, as French fries and potato chips, is increasing, many of the traditional potato dishes are still prepared in Swedish homes.

Baked potatoes are increasingly popular, either as an accompaniment to roast meat or as a dish on their own, served with soured cream and whitebait roe.

New potatoes are a real summer delicacy boiled with dill and served with a pat of butter. At Midsummer the very first new potatoes are served with *matjessill* (sweet-pickled herring), soured cream, and chopped dill or chives. Matjes herrings are available in many delicatessen shops around the world. Try out the Swedish Midsummer meal, and you will find that it is, in all its simplicity, delicious.

Mashed Potatoes 4 servings

Potatismos

10–12 medium-sized potatoes, about 1
  kg/2¼ lb
water
2 tsp salt per litre/1¾ pts/4¼ cups water
200 ml/7 fl oz/good ¾ milk
2–3 tbs butter
½ tsp salt
¼ tsp white or black pepper

Peel and slice the potatoes. Boil in lightly salted water until tender, about 15 min. Drain. Mash the potatoes, using a potato masher or an electric beater.

Heat the milk. Add the milk and the butter to the potato purée. Stir vigorously with a wooden spoon or fork. Season with salt and pepper.

Variation: *Mashed Potatoes with
Green Herbs*   *Grönt potatismos*

Add about 100 ml (3½ fl oz/½ cup) finely chopped green herbs, for instance dill, parsley, and chives to the mashed potatoes just before serving.

Potato Pancakes 4 servings

Raggmunk

8–10 medium-sized raw potatoes, about
  750 g/1⅔ lb
120 g/4 oz/good ¾ cup flour
1½ tsp salt
500 ml/18 fl oz/good 2 cups milk
2 eggs
butter or pork dripping

Mix the flour with the salt and a little of the milk to a smooth batter. Add the rest of the milk and the eggs. Peel and grate the potatoes. Add them to the batter. Heat butter or dripping in a frying pan. Spoon in the batter and spread it out to form thin pancakes. Cook on both sides until crisp. Serve with lingonberry jam and fried bacon.

Potato Cakes 4 servings

Potatisbullar

*10–12 medium-sized potatoes, about 1
    kg/2¼ lb*
water
2 tsp salt per litre/1¾ pts/4¼ cups water
2 eggs
1 tbs butter
1 tsp salt
¼ tsp white or black pepper
grated nutmeg
25–50 g/1–2 oz/¼–½ cup breadcrumbs

Peel and slice the potatoes. Boil them in lightly salted water until tender, about 15 min. Drain.

Mash the potatoes, using a potato masher or an electric beater. Blend in eggs, butter, salt, pepper, and nutmeg. Form into round flat cakes. Coat with breadcrumbs.

Heat a little butter in a frying pan and fry the potato cakes, a few at a time, on both sides.

Serve with lingonberry jam, fried bacon or gammon, and a raw vegetable salad.

Variation: *Potato Pancakes*   *Potatisplättar*

Omit the butter in the recipe above. Add 3 tbs flour and 300 ml (½ pt/1¼ cups) milk. Spoon the batter into the frying pan to form small pancakes, appr. 7½ cm (3 in) in diameter. Serve as described in the recipe above.

Potato Crêpes 4 servings

Rårakor

*10–12 medium-sized potatoes, about 1
    kg/2¼ lb*
1½ tsp salt
butter or pork dripping

Peel the potatoes and grate them, using the large holes of the grater. Drain off liquid. Add salt.

Heat butter or dripping in a frying pan.

Spoon the mixture into the pan and spread out thinly. Cook on both sides until brown and crisp.

Serve with lingonberry jam and bacon.

Potato Waffles 4 servings

Potatisvåfflor

4 medium-sized cold boiled potatoes
400 ml/14 fl oz/1⅔ cups milk
300 g/10 oz/good 2 cups flour
1 tsp baking powder
50 g/1¾ oz/scant ¼ cup butter
200 ml/7 fl oz/good ¾ cup cold water

Mash or rice the potatoes. Mix with the milk. Blend in the flour, mixed with the baking powder. Melt the butter. Stir butter and cold water into the mixture.

Heat the waffle-iron. Cook the waffles and serve with bacon and lingonberry jam or with raw grated carrots.

Thin crisp potato crêpes with bacon.

Potato Cake with Raw Potatoes   4 servings   *Potatiskaka*

8–10 medium-sized potatoes, about
  750 g / 1⅔ lb
1 onion
1 tsp salt
¼ tsp white or black pepper
1–2 packets of bacon, about 150 g
  (5–6 oz) each

Peel the potatoes and grate them, using large holes of grater. Peel and chop the onion. Mix potatoes, onion, salt, and pepper.

Fry the bacon and drain on paper towels.

Turn the potato mixture into a moderately hot frying pan with a little bacon dripping.

Flatten the mixture to form a cake. Cover and cook on low heat for 5–8 min. Loosen the potato cake around the edges and turn it upside down on to a lid or a plate. Add some bacon dripping to the pan and slide the potato cake back into the pan cooked side up. Cover and cook until potatoes are tender and nicely browned, about 5 min.

Arrange the bacon on top of the potato cake and heat through. Serve straight from the pan with a raw vegetable salad.

Potato Waffles with Grated Potatoes 4 servings *Revvåfflor*

8–10 medium-sized potatoes, about
   750 g/1⅔ lb
125 g/4 ½ oz/good cup fine rye flour
60 g/2 oz/scant ½ cup plain white flour
50 g/1¾ oz/scant ½ cup barley flour
or 225 g/8 oz/scant 2 cups
   4-grains bread flour (a mixture of
   wheat, rye, barley, and oats)
1½ tsp salt
300 ml/½ pt/1¼ cups milk butter

Peel the potatoes and grate them, using large holes of grater. Mix with the different kinds of flour or with the bread flour, salt and milk.
Heat the waffle-iron. Butter it.
Cook the waffles and serve with bacon, lingonberry jam, and a raw vegetable salad.

Potato Dumplings from Öland 4 servings *Öländska kroppkakor*

10–12 medium-sized potatoes, about 1
   kg/2¼ lb
5 medium-sized boiled potatoes
90–120 g/3–4½ oz/⅔-good
   ¾ cup flour
1½ tsp salt

Filling:
200 g/7 oz lightly salted bacon
1 onion
½ tsp ground allspice

Boiling:
water
1½ tsp salt per litre/1¾ pts/4¼ cups
   water

Peel and finely grate the raw potatoes.
Drain potatoes carefully in a strainer.
Mash, rice, or grate the boiled potatoes. Mix raw and boiled potatoes, flour, and salt to form a dough.
Dice the bacon. Peel and chop the onion.
Brown the bacon and onion in a frying pan on moderate heat.
Shape dough into a sausage. Cut in 12 pieces and make a hollow in the middle of each.
Place 1 tbs filling in each piece of dough. Close up around the filling and form into balls.
Add some flour to the dough if it seems too sticky.
Bring plenty of water to the boil in a large saucepan. Add salt.
Drop in the dumplings and boil for about 25 min.
Serve with melted butter and lingonberry jam.

White Potato Dumplings 4 servings *Vita kroppkakor*

10 medium-sized cold boiled potatoes
1 egg
150 g/5 oz/good cup flour
about 2 tsp salt

Filling:
200 g/7 oz bacon (salted or smoked)
1 small onion
¼–½ tsp crushed or ground allspice

Boiling:
water
1½ tsp salt per litre/1¾ pts/4¼ cups
   water

Filling: Dice the bacon finely. Peel and chop the onion. Brown bacon and onion lightly in a frying pan. Season with allspice. Set aside to cool.
Mash or rice the potatoes. Mix with egg and flour. Season with salt.
Shape the dough into a sausage. Cut in 12 pieces and make a hollow in the middle of each.
Place 1 tbs of filling in each piece of dough. Close up around the filling, form into balls, and flatten them a little.
Heat plenty of water in a large saucepan. Add salt. When the water boils, drop in the dumplings. Boil until they rise to the surface and then for another 5 min.
Serve with lingonberry jam and a little melted butter (optional).

Potato Dumplings are popular in several regions. Here (clockwise from the top): Potato Dumplings from Öland, from Piteå, and White Potato Dumplings.

Potato Dumplings from Piteå 4 servings *Pitepalt*

10–12 medium-sized potatoes, about 1 kg/2¼ lb
80 g/3 oz/good ¾ cup barley flour
120 g/4 oz/good ¾ cup plain white flour
2 tsp salt

Filling:
200 g/7 oz lightly salted bacon
1 large onion

Boiling:
water
1½ tsp salt per litre/1¾ pts/4¼ cups water

Peel and finely grate the potatoes. Drain thoroughly in a strainer. Mix potatoes, flour, and salt to a soft dough.
Dice the bacon finely. Peel and chop the onion. Form the dough into balls. Add flour if the dough seems too sticky.
Make a hollow in the centre of each dumpling and fill with bacon and onion. Close up the dough around the filling.
Simmer the dumplings very slowly in lightly salted water for about 1 hour.
Serve with melted butter and lingonberry jam.

Potato Cake with Boiled Potatoes 4 servings *Potatiskaka med kokt potatis*

8 medium-sized cold boiled potatoes
1 onion or leek
4 eggs
1–1½ tsp salt
½ tsp white or black pepper
2 tbs butter

Grate the potatoes, using large holes of grater. Peel and chop the onion or rinse and shred the leek. Mix potatoes, onion, eggs, salt, and pepper.
Brown 1 tbs butter in a frying pan. Spread the mixture evenly in the pan and fry on low heat for about 8 min.
Turn out the cake on to a lid or plate. Melt the rest of the butter and slide the potato cake back into the pan, cooked side up. Cook for another 5 min.
Serve with lingonberry jam and bacon or fried gammon.

Creamed Potatoes 4 servings *Råstuvad potatis*

10–12 medium-sized potatoes, about 1 kg/2½ lb
400–500 ml/14–18 fl oz/1⅔-good 2 cups milk
2 tsp salt
¼ tsp white or black pepper
grated nutmeg (optional)
50 ml/3 rounded tbs chopped dill or parsley

Peel and dice the potatoes. Place in a saucepan with enough milk barely to cover them. Add salt, pepper, and optional nutmeg. Cover and simmer on low heat until the potatoes are tender. Stir from time to time. Add more milk if needed. Allow a cooking-time of 20 min. Sprinkle with dill or parsley.
Serve as an accompaniment to smoked meat, fried or grilled sausages, smoked or marinated fish.

Potato Croquettes 4 servings

8–10 medium-sized potatoes, about
    750 g/1⅔ lb
water
2 tsp salt per litre/1¾ pts/4¼ cups water
2 tbs butter
1 egg
1 tsp salt
¼ tsp white or black pepper

Coating:
60 g/2 oz/scant ½ cup flour
1 egg
50 g/1¾ oz/scant ½ cup breadcrumbs

Deep-frying:
Cooking oil

Peel and slice the potatoes. Boil in lightly salted water until tender, about 15 min. Drain.

Mash the potatoes with a potato masher or an electric beater.

Blend in butter and egg. Season with salt and pepper. (N.B. Do not add any liquid!) Set aside to cool.

Form the mixture into balls or cylinders. Beat the egg for the coating. Dredge the qroquettes with flour, dip in egg, and finally coat with breadcrumbs.

Heat the oil to 175°C/350°F. If no thermometer is available, you may check the temperature by dropping a piece of white bread into the oil. If the bread is golden brown after 1 min. the temperature is right.

Deep-fry the croquettes in the oil until nicely browned, about 2 min.

Remove with a slotted spoon and drain on paper towels. The croquettes can be made in advance and reheated in the oven.

Serve as an accompaniment to meat or poultry.

Baked Potatoes 4 servings

8 large potatoes, about
    1 kg/2¼ lb

Scrub the potatoes thoroughly. Prick a few holes in the skin with a fork or a skewer.

Put the potatoes directly on the grid bars of the oven shelf. Bake them in a 225°C/435°F oven for 40–50 min., depending on their size.

Make a cross-shaped incision in the skin of each potato and squeeze out a little of its content.

Serve with soured cream and
- chopped onions (red or yellow)
- finely shredded leek
- whitebait roe or large-grained black or red caviar
- anchovy fillets
- smoked meat or sausage

Variation: *Baked Potato Halves*   *Bakad potatis i halvor*
Cut the potatoes in halves. Brush the cut side with melted butter or oil. Sprinkle with ½–1 tsp salt, ¼ tsp white or black pepper, and 1 tbs cumin or 2 tsp thyme.

Bake the potato halves in the oven until tender, 30–40 min. Serve with meat dishes.

Raw Fried Potatoes   4 servings

8–10 medium-sized potatoes, about
750 g / 1⅔ lb
butter
1 tsp salt
¼ tsp white or black pepper

Peel the potatoes and cut them in 1 cm / ½ in dice or thin slices. Heat the butter in a frying pan and fry the potatoes on low heat, a little at a time, until they are cooked through, 10–12 min. for slices, 12–15 min. for dice.
Serve as accompaniment to fried or roasted meat.

Hasselback Potatoes (Roast Potatoes)

Peel the potatoes. Slice thinly without cutting right through. They should stick together in the bottom.
Arrange the potatoes in a buttered ovenproof dish or a roasting pan.
Brush with melted butter, mixed with salt and pepper. Sprinkle for instance with 100 ml (3½ fl oz / scant ½ cup) grated cheese (optional) or 2 tbs breadcrumbs (optional).
Bake in a 225°C / 435°F oven until tender and browned, about 40 min.

Variation: *Roast Potatoes* (wedges)   *Klyftpotatis*

Peel the potatoes and cut them in wedge-shape. Place in a buttered ovenproof dish or a roasting pan. Brush with melted butter mixed with salt and pepper.
Roast in a 250°C / 480°F oven. Stir and turn the potatoes a couple of times during cooking. Allow a cooking-time of about 20 min. If you wish to prepare roast wedge-potatoes in advance, you may parboil the wedges in lightly salted water (2 tsp salt per litre / 1¾ pts / 4¼ cups water) for 3 min. Drain and roast as described above, but reduce the roasting time to about 15 min.

Swedish Hash   4 servings

8–10 medium-sized potatoes, about
750 g / 1⅔ lb
1 onion
about 400 ml / ¾ pt / 1⅔ cups cooked
beef, finely diced
butter
1 tsp salt
¼ tsp white or black pepper
⅛–¼ tsp ground allspice (optional)

This is an excellent way of using up left-overs. It is a good family dish, but it is just as good for a late-night supper after a party.
Peel and finely dice the potatoes. Peel and chop the onion. Heat the butter in a frying pan and fry the potatoes on low heat, a little at a time, until cooked through, 12–15 min. Remove to a side dish and keep warm.
Separately brown the onion and the meat.
Mix all the ingredients and season with salt and pepper.
Serve at once with fried eggs or raw egg yolks, pickled beetroots, and a raw vegetable salad.

Swedish Hash can also be served with fried eggs.

Buttered Potatoes with Green Herbs 4 servings *Smörskakad grön potatis*

0.75–1 kg/1⅔–2¼ lb new potatoes
water
1 tsp salt per 500 ml/scant pt/good
  2 cups water
2 tbs butter
50 ml/3 rounded tbs each finely
  chopped parsley and dill

Scrub and rinse the potatoes. Bring water and salt to the boil.
Add the potatoes and boil on low heat until tender, about 15 min. Drain and dry off. Remove the potatoes.
Melt the butter in the saucepan. Roll the potatoes in the butter.
Add dill and parsley and shake the pan so that the herbs are evenly distributed on the potatoes.
Serve with herring or with smoked meat.

Potato Salad with Sour-cream Dressing 4 servings

Potatissallad med gräddfilsås

8–10 cold boiled potatoes
1 small cucumber
2 bunches radishes
100 ml/3½ fl oz/scant ½ cup chopped
  chives

Sour-cream Dressing:
200–300 ml/7–10 fl oz/¾–1¼ cups
  soured cream
2–3 tbs prepared mustard
3 tbs chopped pickled
  cucumbers
¼ tsp salt
¼ tsp white or black pepper

Dice the potatoes. Rinse the vegetables. Cut the cucumber in sticks and slice the radishes.
Arrange potatoes, cucumber, radishes, and chives in alternate layers in a serving bowl.
Mix the soured cream with the mustard, pickled cucumbers, salt, and pepper.
Pour the sauce over the salad.
Serve as accompaniment to meat or sausages.

Potato Salad Vinaigrette 4 servings *Potatissallad med vinägrettsås*

8–10 cold boiled potatoes
1 apple
1 pickled cucumber
50 ml/3 rounded tbs chopped green
  herbs, eg. dill and parsley.

Sauce Vinaigrette:
3 tbs salad oil
1 tbs water
2 tbs vinegar
¼ tsp salt
¼ tsp white or black pepper
2 tsp prepared mustard (optional)

Cut the potatoes in slices or dice. Rinse and core the apple. Dice finely. Chop the pickled cucumber. Blend oil, water, and vinegar. Season with salt, pepper, and optional mustard. Arrange potatoes, apple, cucumber, and green herbs in alternate layers in a serving bowl. Pour on the dressing.
Serve as accompaniment to meat or sausages.

Vegetables

The vegetables used in traditional Swedish food are those that are suited to the harsh Swedish climate and can be stored for long periods. Some wild plants have also been used, eg. nettles.

To prepare for the long Swedish winter, broad beans were dried, string beans were salted, carrots, turnips, onions, beetroots, and parsnips were stored in cellars. In this way variation and nourishment in the diet was ensured the year round.

Nowadays there is a strong tendency towards the use of fresh imported vegetables, especially in salads. The traditional Swedish vegetables are, however, both inexpensive and wholesome. They are mostly prepared in simple ways, underlining the special flavour of the vegetable.

Mixed Vegetables may be varied according to the season.

Mixed Vegetables 4 servings

Grönsaksfat

8 small beetroots
8 small carrots
8 fresh onions
200–300 g/7–10 oz sugar peas
  (snow peas) or French beans
water
2 tsp salt per litre/1¾ pts/4¼ cups water

Lemon Butter:
75–100 g/2½–3½ oz/⅓-scant ½ cup
  butter
1 tbs lemon juice

Cut off the beetroot tops, leaving about 5 cm (2 in) of stalks. Do not cut off the root tips. The beetroots will bleed if cut and this impaires their flavour. Scrub the beetroots well. Put them in boiling salted water and boil until tender, 20–30 min.
Test with a fork.
Wash and peel carrots and onions.
Wash and trim peas or beans. Remove strings. Put the vegetables, separately, in boiling salted water and boil until barely tender, 10–15 min. Test with a fork.
Lemon Butter: Cream the butter. Season with lemon juice.
Arrange the vegetables in groups on a serving dish or in separate bowls. Serve with the lemon butter.

Creamed Vegetables 4 servings

Lättstuvade grönsaker

500 g/1 lb 2 oz vegetables, eg. sugar
  peas (snow peas) or string beans cut
  in pieces, shredded cabbage, cauli-
  flower divided into little flowerets,
  small new carrots, sliced carrots,
  parsnips cut in strips
water
2 tsp salt per litre/1¾ pts/4¼ cups water
1 tbs butter
2 tbs flour
300 ml/½ pt/1¼ cups liquid
  (cooking liquid+milk
  +cream)
½ tsp salt
¼ tsp white or black pepper
chopped parsley

Boil the vegetables seperately in lightly salted water until barely tender, 5–10 min. Drain. Save the cooking-liquid.
Melt the butter in a saucepan. Blend in the flour. Thin with the liquid, little by little. Simmer on low heat for 3–5 min., stirring from time to time.
Add the vegetables and mix gently.
Season with salt and pepper. Sprinkle with parsley.

Creamed Spinach 4 servings

Stuvad spenat

375 g/13 oz fresh spinach leaves or
  1 packet frozen chopped spinach,
  about 375 g/13 oz
water
2 tsp salt per litre/1¾ pts/4¼ cups water
2 tbs butter
2 tbs flour
200 ml/7 fl oz/good ¾ cup milk
½–1 tsp salt
¼ tsp white or black pepper
⅛ tsp grated nutmeg

Wash the spinach and remove any thick stems. Blanch in lightly salted water, 2–3 min. Cool the spinach under running cold water and drain well. Chop finely.
If frozen spinach is used, thaw lightly.
Melt the butter in a saucepan. Add the spinach and cook for a minute or two. Mix flour and milk together and stir it into the spinach.
Boil for 3–5 min. stirring from time to time.
Season with salt, pepper, and nutmeg.

Creamed Cabbage may be served with fried slices of Falu sausage, Frankfurters, or knockwurst.

Broad Beans in White Sauce   4 servings

Stuvade bondbönor

1.5 kg/3⅓ lb broad beans in their pods
or about 400 g/14 oz/2½ cups
shelled beans
2 carrots (optional)
water
2 tsp salt per litre/1¾ pts/4¼ cups water
2 tbs butter
3 tbs flour
500 ml/18 fl oz/good 2 cups liquid
(cooking liquid + milk)
½ tsp salt
¼ tsp white or black pepper
chopped parsley

Shell and rinse the beans. Peel and slice the carrots. Boil the beans in lightly salted water for about 30 min. Add the optional carrots when appr. 15 min. remains of the cookingtime.
Melt the butter in a saucepan. Blend in the flour. Thin with cooking liquid and milk. Simmer for 3–5 min., stirring from time to time.
Add beans and carrots and mix gently. Season with salt and pepper. Sprinkle with parsley.

Peas in the Pod   4 servings

Släpärter

1 kg/2¼ lb young pods of green peas or
field peas
water
2 tsp salt per litre/1¾ pts/4¼ cups water
75–100 g/3–4 oz/⅓–½ cup butter

Rinse the peas well, but do not trim them. Put them in boiling salted water. Boil until tender, 15–30 min., the cooking-time depends on their freshness. Drain. Melt the butter in a saucepan. Serve the peas with the melted butter handed separately.
This is the way to eat peas in the pod:
Pick up the pod by its top with your fingers. Dip in the melted butter. Drag the pod between your teeth, so that only the tough membrane is left.

Parsnips au Gratin   4 servings

Ostgratinerade palsternackor

4 parsnips, about 400 g/14 oz
water
2 tsp salt per litre/1¾ pts/4¼ cups water

Sauce:
1½ tbs butter
3 tbs flour
400 ml/14 fl oz/1¾ cups milk
200–300 ml/7–10 fl oz/¾–1¼ cups
grated cheese
½ tsp salt
pinch of white or black pepper

Peel the parsnips and cut them in 1 cm (½ in) slices. Boil in lightly salted water for about 10 min. Drain. Place the parsnips in an ovenproof dish.
Melt the butter in a saucepan. Blend in the flour and thin with the milk. Let the sauce simmer for 3–5 min.
Blend in the grated cheese and season with salt and pepper. Pour the sauce over the parsnips.
Brown in a 250°C/480°F oven for about 10 min.

Root Vegetables au Gratin   4 servings   *Rotsaksgratäng*

1 turnip, about 750 g/1 ⅔ lb
3–4 carrots
4 potatoes
1 leek
water
2 tsp salt per litre/1¾ pts/4¼ cups water
300 ml/½ pt/1¼ cups grated cheese
100 ml/3½ fl oz/scant ½ cup cream

Peel the turnip and the potatoes. Scrape the carrots. Rinse the leek. Cut the vegetables into thin slices.
Put the turnip and the carrots in a saucepan. Measure the water and pour in enough barely to cover the vegetables. Add salt. Boil for 10 min. Add the potatoes and the leek. Boil for another 10 min. Remove the vegetabels. (Save the cooking-liquid for soup.) Arrange the vegetables and the grated cheese in alternate layers in a buttered ovenproof dish. The top layer should be cheese. Pour in the cream.
Brown in a 225°C/435°F oven until the cheese has melted and browned, about 20 min.
Serve with smoked or salted meat.

Variation: *Root Vegetable Casserole*   *Rotsakslåda*
Substitute 6 potatoes, 3 parsnips, 3 carrots, and 3 tbs chopped parsley for the vegetables used in the master recipe.
Peel the vegetables. Cut into thin slices. Arrange in alternate layers with parsley and cheese in an ovenproof dish. Pour in 200 ml (7 fl oz/good ¾ cup) cream.
Bake in a 225°C/435°F oven until the vegetables are tender, about 45 min.

Cauliflower with Chopped Eggs   4 servings   *Kokt blomkål med äggfräs*

1 large cauliflower, about 800 g/1¾ lb
water
2 tsp salt per litre/1¾ pts/4¼ cups water
3–4 hard-boiled eggs
1 tbs butter
100 ml/3½ fl oz/scant ½ cup finely
   chopped green herbs (parsley, dill,
   and chives)

Wash and trim the cauliflower. Some of the green leaves may be left on.
Boil the cauliflower in lightly salted water until tender, about 15 min.
Peel and chop the eggs. Melt the butter in a saucepan. Fry the eggs for a couple of minutes. Add the green herbs.
Take out the cauliflower, drain, and place on a serving dish. Pour the egg mixture over it.

Sautéed Celeriac (Celery-root)   4 servings   *Selleribiffar*

1 celeriac, about 500 g/1 lb 2 oz
water
2 tsp salt per litre/1¾ pts/4¼ cups water
1 egg
3 tbs breadcrumbs
butter

Peel the celeriac and cut it in 1 cm (½ in) slices. Boil in lightly salted water until barely tender, about 10 min. Drain well. Dip the slices in beaten egg, then coat with breadcrumbs. Heat a little butter in a frying pan. Fry the 'steaks' on low heat until nicely browned, about 5 min. each side.
Serve with fried onions or mushroom sauce (see page 62) and boiled potatoes.

Mashed Turnips 4 servings

Rotmos

1 large turnip, about 750 g/1⅔ lb
3 carrots
6–8 potatoes
stock or lightly salted water
    (2 tsp salt per litre/1¾ pts/
    4¼ cups water)
50 ml/3 rounded tbs finely chopped
    parsley

Peel the vegetables and slice them.
Bring the liquid to the boil. Add the turnips and the carrots,
Boil for about 30 min.
Add the potatoes and boil until all the vegetables are tender, about 15 min.
Pour away the cooking-liquid, but save some to thin the purée. Mash the vegetables, using a Moulinette, a masher, or an electric beater. Thin with a little cooking-liquid. Season with salt and pepper if needed. Sprinkle with parsley.
Serve with boiled salted meat.
The vegetables may also be boiled together with meat. In this case turnips and carrots are added when 45 min. cooking-time remains for the meat and the potatoes are added 30 min later.

Swedish Brown Beans 4 servings

Bruna bönor

320 g/12 oz/1⅔ cups red kidney beans
water
2 tsp salt per litre/1¾ pts/4¼ cups water
about 2 tbs vinegar
about 2 tbs treacle (molasses) or sugar

Soak the beans in water, for instance overnight. Discard the soaking water. Place the beans in a large saucepan. Measure the water and pour in enough to cover the beans. Add salt. Simmer until tender, about 1–1½ hours. Season with vinegar, treacle or sugar, and if needed some more salt.
The beans can also be cooked without soaking. Rinse them and boil in 1.5 l (2⅔ pts/6⅓ cups) water and 1 tbs salt. Allow about 2 hours' cooking-time.
Proceed as described above.
Serve with fried bacon or sausages.

Creamed Mushrooms 4 servings

Gräddstuvad svamp

about 1 l/1¾ pts/4¼ cups fresh mush-
    rooms, cleaned and trimmed or
    about 200 g/7 oz tinned or frozen
    mushrooms
2 tbs butter
1 tbs flour
300 ml/½ pt/1¼ cups cream
½ tsp salt
¼ tsp white or black pepper

Cut the mushrooms in pieces. Melt half the butter in a saucepan. Add the mushrooms. Fry until all liquid has evaporated. Add the rest of the butter. Blend in the flour. Thin with the cream. Simmer on low heat for about 10 min, stirring from time to time. Season with salt and pepper.

Variation: *Mushroom Sauce:*
Add 100 ml (3½ fl oz/scant ½ cup) milk, water, or juice from tinned mushrooms.
Proceed as described above.

Many different species of mushrooms are found in the forests. The Swedes like them creamed, added to stews, or served as accompaniment to meat and fish dishes.

Egg dishes and the like

Eggs have always been important, and are even more so today, because of their flavour, their nutritional value, and their role in many cooking techniques. In view of their nutritional value and usefulness eggs are also cheap.

In the old days eggs were scarce during the dark season, when the hens stopped laying. This made eggs an appreciated spring primeur.

Nowadays eggs are used on the same scale all the year round, except at Easter, when the Swedes eat lots of them.

Eggs and milk are the main ingredients in many popular Swedish dishes—pancakes, *plättar*, omelets, and gratins.

Thin Pancakes or Crepes 4 servings *Tunna pannkakor*

3 eggs
550–600 ml/about 1 pt/
2⅓–2½ cups milk
150 g/5¼ oz/good cup flour
½ tsp salt
3 tbs melted butter

Beat the eggs with a little of the milk. Blend in the flour and the salt and beat until the batter is smooth. Add the rest of the milk and the melted butter.

Make thin pancakes in a frying pan or a crêpe pan. A little extra butter in the pan may be needed for the first pancake. Serve the pancakes with jam and for instance a salad.

Variation: *Plättar*
Follow the recipe above, but make small blini-sized (7 cm/ 3 in diam.) pancakes on a special griddle, in blini pans, or in an ordinary frying pan.

Variation: *Batter Pudding*   *Ungspannkaka*
Follow the recipe for thin pancakes above, but pour the batter into a buttered roasting pan, about 30 × 40 cm (12 × 16 in). Bake in a 225°C/435°F oven for about 30 min.

Variation: *Bacon Pancake*   *Fläskpannkaka i ugn*
Cut 150–200 g (5–7 oz) salted or smoked bacon into strips. Brown the bacon in a roasting pan in a 225°C/435°F oven for about 10 min. Proceed as for Batter Pudding above, but omit the butter. Pour the batter over the bacon in the roasting pan. Bake.

Variation: *Batter Pudding with Apples*   *Äppelpannkaka i ugn*
Follow the recipe for Batter Pudding above. Add thin slices or wedges of 2–3 peeled and cored apples to the batter in the pan. Sprinkle with a mixture of 3 tbs sugar and 1 tsp cinnamon. Bake.

Egg Waffles   appr. 10 rounds

Äggvåfflor

50 g/1¾ oz/scant ¼ cup butter
3 eggs
300 ml/½ pt/1¼ cups milk
180 g/6⅓ oz/1¼ cups flour
1½ tsp baking powder
100 ml/3½ fl oz/scant ½ cup whipping
   cream

Melt the butter. Beat the eggs with half the milk and the flour mixed with the baking powder to a smooth batter. Add the cool melted butter and the rest of the milk.

Whip the cream and fold it gently into the batter.

Heat the waffle iron. Cook the waffles until nicely browned. Cool on a rack.

Serve with soured cream mixed with Swedish caviar and chopped dill, or with chopped Swedish anchovy fillets and chives.

Or serve them as a sweet with jam and whipped cream (optional).

This plätt *griddle is a museum piece. Nowadays the griddle is made to take seven* plättar.

Open Omelet, Swedish Style 4 servings

Äggakaka

5 eggs
400 ml / 14 fl oz / 1⅔ cups milk
60 g / 2 oz / scant ½ cup flour
½ tsp salt

Beat the eggs with a little of the milk. Add the flour and continue beating until the batter is smooth. Add the rest of the milk and the salt. Heat a little butter in a frying pan, pour in the batter, and cook on moderate heat. Lift the batter with a fork, so that it sets evenly.

Invert the omelet on to a plate or a lid. Slide it back into the frying pan and cook the other side until evenly browned. Serve the omelet with fried apple slices, apple sauce, or lingonberry jam.

Variation: *Bacon Omelet*

Äggakaka med fläsk

Fry 200 g / 7 oz sliced salted bacon until crisp. Drain on paper towels and keep hot while you prepare the omelet as described above.

Arrange the bacon on top of the omelet.
Serve with a salad and lingonberry jam (optional).

Open Omelet with Bacon.

Filled Pancakes 4 servings

3 eggs
300 ml/½ pt/1¼ cups milk or cream and
milk
60 g/2 oz/scant ½ cup flour
½ tsp salt
2 tbs melted butter
50 ml/3 rounded tbs grated cheese

Beat the eggs with a little of the milk. Add the flour and the salt and continue beating until the batter is smooth. Add the rest of the milk and the melted butter. Make small thin pancakes in a crêpe pan or a small frying pan. A little extra butter in the pan may be needed for the first pancake. Place the cooked pancake on a flat surface. Put the filling in a band across the pancake. Roll up and arrange the rolls close together in an ovenproof dish. Sprinkle with cheese.

Suggested Fillings:
- Creamed Mushrooms (see page 62)
- shellfish ragout
- mussels cooked in butter with shredded leek and chopped parsley
- fried mushrooms with shredded ham or left-over meat and chopped onion
- finely cut smoked ham with chopped chives and a little soured cream

Brown the pancakes in a 250°C/480°F oven for 8–10 min.

Variation: *Mound of Pancakes*   *Pannkakstårta*
Follow the recipe above. Make thin pancakes and leave to cool on a flat surface.
Whip 200 ml (7 fl oz/good ¾ cup) cream.
Pile the pancakes with whipped cream and fresh or thawed berries between them. Decorate with whipped cream and berries.

Country Style Omelet 4 servings

100 g/3½ oz smoked ham
3–4 cold boiled potatoes
1 small onion
butter
4 eggs
4–6 tbs water
½ tsp salt
¼ tsp white or black pepper
chopped parsley

Dice the ham and the potatoes. Peel and chop the onion. Heat a little butter in a frying pan and fry the onion. Add potatoes and ham and cook for a couple of minutes.
Beat the eggs with the water, salt, and pepper. Pour on to the potato-ham mixture in the pan. Lift the batter with a fork, so that it may set evenly.
Cook until the omelet is barely set. It should be soft and creamy.
Turn out on to a serving dish or serve straight from the pan.
Sprinkle with parsley.

Baked Omelet 4 servings

600 ml/good pint/2½ cups milk
4 eggs
1 tbs flour
1 tsp salt
¼ tsp white or black pepper

Garnish:
Creamed spinach or creamed mushrooms, asparagus or parsnips in white sauce (see page 58 and page 62).

Scald the milk and leave to cool.
Beat eggs and flour together. Add milk, salt, and pepper.
Pour the batter into a buttered ovenproof dish.
Bake in a 200°C/400°F oven until the omelet is set and the top is browned, about 20 min.
Cover the omelet with one of the suggested garnishes.

Variation: *Baked Custard*   *Äggstanning*
Follow the above recipe, but use only 400 ml (14 fl oz/1⅔ cups) milk and omit the flour.

Egg and Caviar Gratin 4 servings

4–6 hard-boiled eggs
150 ml/¼ pt/⅔ cup whipping cream
1 small tube Swedish caviar, about 100 g/3½ oz
2 tbs finely chopped dill
100 ml/1½ oz/scant ½ cup grated cheese

Peel and slice the eggs. Arrange in a buttered ovenproof dish. Whip the cream and mix it with caviar and dill. Spread over the eggs. Sprinkle with the grated cheese.
Brown in a 250°C/480°F oven for about 10 min.
Serve with a salad.

Variation: *Egg and Anchovy Gratin*   *Ägglåda med ansjovis och lök*
Follow the above recipe, but substitue 1 small tin of Swedish anchovy fillets, about 50 g (1¾ oz) and 1 onion for the caviar and dill. Chop the anchovy fillets. Peel, chop, and fry the onion.
Mix chopped anchovies and onion with the whipped cream. Proceed as described above.

Macaroni Pudding 4 servings

800–1000 ml/1½–1¾ pt/3⅓–4¼ cups boiled macaroni
1 small onion or 100 ml/3½ fl oz/scant ½ cup finely shredded leek
3 eggs
300 ml/½ pt/1¼ cups milk
1 tsp salt
¼ tsp white or black pepper

Peel and chop the onion. Heat a little butter in a frying pan and cook the onion or leek until soft. Beat eggs, milk, salt, and pepper together.
Place alternate layers of macaroni and onion in a buttered ovenproof dish. Pour in the batter. Bake in a 225°C/435°F oven for 30–40 min.
Serve with a raw vegetable salad.

Variation: *Macaroni Pudding with*
Ham or Sausage   *Makaronipudding med skinka eller korv*
Dice appr. 200 g/7 oz smoked ham, smoked pork loin, or Falu sausage into dice. Alternate with macaroni and onion in the dish. Omit the salt in the batter. Proceed as described above.

Desserts

Many modern Swedes see the dessert as an unnecessary and fattening luxury. This is unfortunate, because most Swedish desserts are light and refreshing. But even those who have stopped serving cooked desserts still put a bowl of fresh fruit on the table to end the meal.

Swedes love fruit, especially soft fruit and there are many varieties to choose from, wild as well as cultivated. They are eaten fresh when in season and are frozen or made into fruit syrup for winter use. The fresh or frozen berries are often served with whipped cream or vanilla cream sauce.

Fruit syrup can be used for refreshing drinks, but it is also the basic ingredient in many desserts. It is thickened with potato flour to make fruit soup or fruit cream. The wild rose hips are often dried and then made into a delicious and vitamin-rich soup.

Cloudberries, which grow in the northern regions, make a delicious jam, often served with pancakes or ice cream.

To Swedes in general, the most important of all berries are the lingonberries (red whortleberries). They are usually made into jam, which is served with pancakes and other desserts, but also with various meat dishes.

Apples and pears are used in tarts, and the traditional apple cake is a Swedish version of the English Brown Betty.

Set Soured Milk   3–4 servings   *Filbunke*

500 ml/scant pint/good 2 cups regular milk
100 ml/3 ½ fl oz/scant ½ cup soured milk

Heat the milk to just below boiling point (to prevent the soured milk from separating). Cool the milk to normal room temperature, 22°C/72°F. Mix in the soured milk.

Pour into individual bowls. Cover and leave until set, for instance overnight. Chill.

Serve with gingerbread bisquits, ground ginger, or fresh fruit.

Beestings Pudding 4–6 servings

Kalvdans av råmjölk

1 l/1¾ pts/4¼ cups diluted beestings
(raw milk)
1 tbs sugar
¼ tsp salt
1 tsp ground cardamom, cinnamon, or
10 almonds, blanched, skinned, and
chopped

Garnish:
jam or soft fruit

Beestings or raw milk is obtained immediately after calving. The concentration varies, depending upon when it was milked. Beestings from the first milking must be thinned down with twice its quantity of ordinary milk (0.5 l beestings + 1 l milk), or the pudding will become too hard. Beestings from later milkings can be thinned down with an equal quantity of ordinary milk.

Mix beestings, sugar, salt, and spices or almonds together. Pour into a buttered 1.5 l (2½ pts/6 cups) ovenproof dish or mould. Place the mould in a tin of boiling water in the lower part of a preheated 175°C/350°F oven and bake until the pudding has set and the top browned, 30–45 min. Serve lukewarm or cold with jam or soft fruit.

Variation: *Beestings Pudding from
Ordinary Milk*

Kalvdans utan råmjölk

Replace the beestings in the above recipe with 750 ml (1⅓ pts/scant 3¼ cups) ordinary milk. Add 1 bag of milk powder (sufficient for 1 l/1¾ pts/4¼ cups milk). Beat in 2 eggs. Omit the sugar. Proceed as described in the master recipe.

Caramel Custard 4 servings

Brylépudding

300 ml/½ pt/1¼ cups milk
100 ml/3½ fl oz/scant ½ cup cream
4 eggs
grated rind of ½ lemon (carefully
washed)

For the mould:
170 g/6 oz/good ¾ cup sugar
1 tbs boiling water

Start by lining the mould. Melt the sugar in a frying pan on low heat. Scrape the sugar from the bottom of the pan with a wooden spatula. Add the water when the sugar has melted (take care not to burn yourself). Pour the caramel into a mould, appr. 1.5 l (2½ pts/6 cups). Tilt the mould in all directions to film the bottom and sides with caramel.

Bring the milk and the cream to the boiling point in a saucepan or in the pan used for the caramel (which will give caramel colour and flavour to the milk). Beat the eggs. Pour on the milk and cream mixture and mix in the lemon peel. Pour the mixture into the mould.

Place the mould in a tin with boiling water in the lower part of a preheated 200°C/400°F oven.

Bake until set, about 40 min.

Leave the custard to cool before turning out on to a serving dish. Pour over any caramel syrup remaining in the mould. 1 tbs brandy may be added to this sauce.

Rice Pudding 4 servings

1 batch Rice Porridge (see page 158)
2 eggs
200 ml/7 fl oz/good ¾ cup milk
60 g/2 oz/scant ½ cup raisins
35 g/1¼ oz/scant ¼ cup almonds,
  blanched, skinned, and chopped
1 grated bitter almond

To Serve:
jam or soft fruit

Mix the rice porridge with eggs and milk. Add raisins and almonds. Pour the mixture into a buttered ovenproof dish. Bake in a 225°C/435°F oven for about 30 min.
Serve lukewarm with jam or soft fruit.

Variation: *Semolina*
(Cream of Wheat) Pudding   *Mannagrynskaka*
Substitute 1 batch Semolina Porridge (see page 10) for the rice porridge and omit milk and bitter almond. Flavour with grated rind of ½ lemon or ½ orange (optional). Proceed as described above. Serve with Fruit Sauce (see page 82).

Variation: *Saffron Pudding*   *Saffranspannkaka*
Follow the recipe for Rice Pudding, but use 4 eggs. Omit raisins and bitter almond. Add ½ g saffron, dissolved in a little water or milk, and 1 tbs sugar. Bake as above.

Cream Pudding 4 servings

3 egg yolks
2 tbs sugar
3 tbs flour
grated rind of ½ lemon (carefully
  washed)
300 ml/½ pt/1¼ cups whipping cream
3 egg whites

To Serve:
jam or soft fruit

Blend egg yolks, sugar, and flour together. Add the lemon rind. Whip the cream and the egg whites separately. Gently fold first the cream then the egg whites into the egg mixture. Turn into a buttered round ovenproof dish.
Bake in a 175°C/350°F oven for about 45 min.
Serve at once with jam or soft fruit.

Variation: *Cream Pudding with Soured Cream*
Substitute 300 ml (½ pt/1¼ cups) soured cream for the whipping cream. Proceed as described above.

Cheese Cake with Cottage Cheese 5–6 servings

50 g/1¾ oz almonds
2 bitter almonds
3 eggs
40 g/1½ oz/scant ¼ cup sugar
30 g/1 oz/scant ¼ cup flour
500 g/1 lb 2 oz fresh curd cheese, eg.
  cottage cheese
200 ml/7 fl oz/good ¾ cup whipping
  cream

To Serve:
soft fruit or jam
whipped cream

Blanch, skin, and finely chop the almonds.
Beat the eggs with the sugar. Add flour, almonds, and curd cheese.
Whip the cream. Fold into the cheese mixture.
Turn into a buttered ovenproof dish, appr. 1.5 l (2½ pts/6 cups).
Bake in a 175°C/350°F oven until set and browned, about 1 hour.
Leave to cool or chill.
Serve with soft fruit or jam and whipped cream.

Curd Cake 6–8 servings

Ostkaka

4 l/7 pts/4½ quarts milk
60 g/2 oz/scant ½ cup flour
1 tbs cheese rennet
50–75 g/1¾–2¼ oz almonds
3 bitter almonds
4 eggs
400 ml/¾ pt/1 ⅔ cups cream
50 g/1¾ oz/good ¼ cup sugar

To Serve:
Soft fruit or jam
whipped cream

Curd Cake is normally made according to regional recipes. The curd cake shown here has been baked in an old copper mould.

Mix 300 ml (½ pt/1¼ cups) of the milk with the flour in a bowl. Warm the rest of the milk in a saucepan to just under blood heat, 35°C/95°F. Away from the heat, blend in the flour-mixture and the rennet. Cover and let stand for about 30 min.

Blanch, skin, and finely chop the almonds. Butter an oven-proof dish, appr. 2 l (3½ pts/8½ cups).

Cut the curds to facilitate draining. Stir gently with a wooden fork.

Pour the curds into a colander lined with cheesecloth. Leave to drain.

Squeeze the cheesecloth a little to help extract the whey.

Beat the eggs with cream and sugar. Blend in the curd cheese and the almonds. Pour into the dish.

Bake in a 175°C/350°F oven until browned and set, 1–1¼ hours. Leave to cool or chill.

Serve with soft fruit or jam and whipped cream.

Bread Fritters 4 servings

Fattiga riddare

8 thin slices of white bread
50 ml/1¾ fl oz/scant ¼ cup apple sauce
100–150 ml/3½–5 fl oz/scant ½–⅔ cup
* milk*
butter
2 tbs sugar
1 tsp ground cinnamon

Sandwich the bread slices together two and two around the apple sauce. Dip in milk.
Heat the butter in a frying pan and fry on moderate heat until brown and crisp, about 3 min. each side.
Mix sugar and cinnamon. Turn the hot fritters in this mixture.
Serve with apple sauce.

Crisp Waffles 8 rounds

Frasvåfflor

2 tbs butter
200 ml/7 fl oz/good ¾ cup water
180 g/6⅓ oz/1¼ cups flour
300 ml/½ pt/1¼ cups whipping cream

To Serve:
jam
whipped cream (optional)

Melt the butter and leave to cool. Mix the water and flour to a smooth batter. Whip the cream. Add the melted butter to the mixture, then fold in the cream.
Heat the waffle iron. Pour a little of the batter on to the iron and cook until golden brown on both sides.
Serve at once with jam and optional whipped cream.

Swedish Apple Cake 4 servings

Äppelkaka

300 g/10 oz/2½ cups grated rye bread
* or white breadcrumbs*
100 g/3½ oz/scant ½ cup butter
4 apples or 300 ml/½ pt/1¼ cups lightly
* sweetened apple purée*
3 rounded tbs/scant ¼ cup brown or
* granulated sugar*

To Serve:
whipped cream

Place the breadcrumbs in a frying pan with the butter and brown on moderate heat, until the crumbs are crisp. Peel and core the apples. Cut them into wedges.
Butter an ovenproof dish. Put in alternate layers of breadcrumbs, apples or apple purée and sugar. The top layer should be breadcrumbs.
Bake in a 200°C/400°F oven for appr. 20 min.
Serve directly from the dish with whipped cream.

Apple Cake with Oats 4 servings

Äppelkaka med havregryn

4 apples
1 tsp ground cinnamon
100 g/3½ oz/scant ½ cup butter
35 g/1¼ oz/scant ½ cup rolled oats
85 g/3 oz/scant ½ cup sugar
2 tbs cream
60 g/2 oz/scant ½ cup flour

To Serve:
whipped cream

Peel and core the apples. Cut them in wedges and place them in a buttered ovenproof dish. Sprinkle with cinnamon.
Mix butter, rolled oats, sugar, and flour in a saucepan. Bring to the boil, stirring. Spread the mixture over the apples.
Bake in a 225°C/435°F oven until the top is browned and the apples tender, 15–20 min. Serve lukewarm with chilled whipped cream.

Fruit Pie 4 servings

Shortcrust Pastry:
180 g/6⅓ oz/1¼ cups flour
125 g/4½ oz/good ½ cup butter
2 tbs water

Rub the butter into the flour until the mixture is crumby. Add the water and mix quickly. Chill for 30 min.

Variation: *Pastry with Semolina*   *Pajdeg med mannagryn*

Mix 90 g (3¼ oz/⅔ cup) flour with 105 g (3¾ oz/⅔ cup) semolina (cream of wheat). Proceed as described above.

Crumble:
120 g/4¼ oz/good ¾ cup flour
45 g/good 1½ oz/scant ¼ cup sugar
100 g/3½ oz/scant ½ cup butter

Mix flour and sugar on your pastry board. Cut or rub the butter into the flour until the mixture is crumby.

Variation: *Crumble with Oats*   *Smuldeg med havregryn*

Mix 60 g (2 oz/scant ½ cup) flour with 50 g (1¾ oz/⅔ cup) rolled oats. Proceed as described above.

Filling:
● *Rhubarb Pie:*
  500 g/1 lb 2 oz rhubarb
  85 g/3 oz/scant ½ cup sugar
  2 tsp potato flour

Rinse and peel the rhubarb. Cut in 1 cm (½ in) pieces.

● *Apple Pie:*
  4 apples
  45 g/good 1½ oz/scant ¼ cup sugar
  1–2 tsp ground cinnamon
  60 g/2 oz/scant ½ cup raisins
  (optional)

Peel, quarter, and core the apples. Cut into thin wedges.

● *Blueberry Pie:*
  500 ml/scant pint/good 2 cups fresh
  blueberries or 1 packet frozen
  blueberries, about 200 g/7 oz
  45 g/good 1½ oz/scant ¼ cup sugar
  1 tsp vanilline sugar or vanilla extract
  1 tsp potato flour

To Serve:
vanilla cream sauce, custard
  sauce
or whipped cream

Serve with Vanilla Cream/Sauce, Custard Sauce (see page 81), or whipped cream.
Roll out ¾ of the shortcrust pastry thinly and line a pie tin or a flan ring.
Bake the shell in a 225°C/435°F oven for about 15 min.
Fill the shell with a mixture of fruit or berries, sugar, optional flavouring, and potato flour.
Roll out the remaining pastry. Cut into thin strips and arrange in lattice fashion over the filling.

Or:
Place fruit or berries, sugar, optional flavouring, and potato flour in an ovenproof dish. Sprinkle the *crumble* over the filling.
Bake the pies in a 225°C/435°F oven until the top is brown and crisp and the fruit is soft, about 20 min.
Serve with vanilla cream sauce, custard sauce (see page 81), or whipped cream.

Apples Baked in Pastry   4 servings   *Äppelknyten*

Shortcrust Pastry:
180 g/6⅓ oz/1¼ cups flour
1 tbs sugar
125 g/scant 4½ oz/good ½ cup butter
2 tbs water

4 small apples
2 tbs sugar
1–2 tsp ground cinnamon

To brush:
beaten egg

To Serve:
custard sauce or whipped cream

Mix flour and sugar on the pastry board. Rub in the butter until the mixture looks like breadcrumbs. Add the water and mix quickly. Chill for 30 min.

Peel and core the apples, using an apple-corer. Mix sugar and cinnamon.

Divide the pastry into four parts. Roll out each part thinly. Place an apple on each round of pastry. Fill the centres of the apples with the sugar mixture. Enclose each apple in pastry. Place on a buttered baking sheet. Brush with beaten egg.

Bake in 200°C/400°F oven until the pastry is browned and the apples tender, 20–30 min.

Serve with custard sauce (see page 81) or whipped cream.

Baked Apples   4 servings   *Stekta äpplen*

6–8 apples
2 tbs sugar
2 tsp cinnamon
2 tbs butter

To Serve:
custard sauce

Rinse the apples and peel them (optional). Core them with an apple corer.

Place the apples in a buttered ovenproof dish.

Mix sugar and cinnamon. Fill the centres of the apples with the sugar mixture. Put a nut of butter on each apple.

Bake the apples in a 225°C/435°F oven until just tender, 20–30 min.

Serve warm with custard sauce (see page 81).

Variation: *Baked Apples with Treacle (molasses)*   *Sirapsäpplen*
Replace the filling with 100 ml (3½ fl oz/scant ½ cup) chopped hazel nuts. Trickle on 2–3 tbs treacle. Proceed as described above.

Apple Soup with Raisins   4 servings   *Äppelsoppa med russin*

4–5 apples
1 l/1¾ pt/4¼ cups water
about 45 g/1½ oz/scant ¼ cup sugar
1 piece of cinnamon
60 g/2 oz/scant ½ cup raisins
1½ tbs potato flour + 50 ml/1¾ fl
oz/scant ¼ cup water
1 tsp lemon juice (optional)

Peel and quarter the apples. Core them and cut into slices. Bring the water to the boil with sugar and cinnamon. Add the apples and the raisins. Simmer until the apples are tender. Mix potato flour and water. Away from the heat stir the thickening into the soup. Bring back to the boiling point.

Season with optional lemon juice.

Serve hot or cold.

Apples Baked in Pastry and Swedish Apple Cake.

Cherry Soup 4 servings

Körsbärssoppa

700–800 ml/1¼–1½ pts/3–3½ cups
  cherry compote
200 ml/7 fl oz/good ¾ cup water

or
500 ml/scant pint/good 2 cups stoned
  cherries
200 ml/7 fl oz/good ¾ cup cherry syrup
600 ml/good pint/2½ cups water

1 piece of cinnamon
1½ tbs potato flour + 50 ml/
  1¾ fl oz/scant ¼ cup water

Mix cherry compote and water or cherries and thinned down syrup in a saucepan. Add cinnamon. Bring to the boil and boil for 2 min.

Mix potato flour and water. Away from the heat stir in the thickening.

Bring back to the boiling point. Allow to cool.

Serve chilled with a few ice cubes.

Fruit Soup with Dried Fruit 4 servings

Fruktsoppa av torkad frukt

1 packet mixed dried fruit (prunes,
  apricots, and apples), about 250 g/9
  oz
1¼ l/2¼ pts/5¼ cups water
1 piece of cinnamon
1½ tbs potato flour + 50 ml/1¾ fl oz/
  scant ¼ cup water
100–200 ml/3½–7 fl oz/½–good ¾ cup
  concentrated fruit syrup, eg. blackcurrant or raspberry

Cut the fruit into small pieces. Place in a saucepan with water and cinnamon.

Cover and simmer on low heat for about 15 min.

Mix potato flour and water. Away from the heat, stir in the thickening. Bring to the boil. Add the fruit syrup. Leave to cool.

N.B. The fruit syrup may be omitted and 45–65 g (1½–2¼ oz/¼–⅓ cup) sugar added at the beginning of the cooking.

Variation: *Prune Soup*   *Sviskonsoppa*
Substitute prunes for the mixed fruit. Simmer for about 10 min. Proceed as described above.

Variation: *Sago Soup*   *Sagosoppa*
Follow the recipe for Fruit Soup, but add 3 rounded tbs pearl sago and use only ½ packet dried fruit. Simmer for about 25 min. Omit the potato flour.

Stewed Prunes 4 servings

Katrinplommonkompott

1 packet stoned prunes, about
  250 g/9 oz
300 ml/½ pt/1¼ cups water
45 g/1½ oz/scant ¼ cup sugar
2 tsp potato flour + 50 ml/1¾ fl oz/scant
  ¼ cup water

Place the prunes in a saucepan with the water. Cover and simmer on low heat for about 5 min. Add the sugar. Mix potato flour and water. Away from the heat, stir in the thickening. Bring back to the boil.

Set aside to cool, or chill.

Serve with light cream or cream mixed with milk.

Rose Hip Soup   4 servings

Nyponsoppa av torkade nypon

300 ml / ½ pt / 1 ¼ cups dried rose hips
1.5 l / 2⅔ pts / 6⅓ cups water
85 g / 3 oz / scant ½ cup sugar
1 tbs potato flour + 50 ml / 1¾ fl oz / scant
  ¼ cup water

Pound the rose hips in a mortar and soak them in the water for some hours. Boil in the soaking water until tender, about 45 min.

Pass through a sieve and add enough water to make appr. 1 l / 1¾ pts / 4¼ cups. Bring to the boil. Add sugar to taste. Mix potato flour and water. Away from the heat, stir in the thickening. Bring back to the boil. Set aside to cool. Serve with rusks or almond biscuits. Whipped cream or ice cream also go very nicely with it.

Variation: *Rose Hip Soup with*
Fresh Rose hips   *Nyponsoppa av färska nypon*

Mix 300 ml (good ½ pint / 1¼ cups) boiled and sieved fresh rose hips (see Rose Hip Purée, page 111) with 700 ml (1¼ pts / 3 cups) water in a saucepan. Bring to the boil. Add sugar to taste and thicken the soup with potato flour as described above.

Apple Compote   4 servings

Äppelkräm

4–6 apples
400 ml / scant ¾ pt / 1⅔ cups water
about 45 g / 1½ oz / ¼ cup sugar
juice of ½ lemon (optional)
2 tbs potato flour + 50 ml / 1¾ fl oz / scant
  ¼ cup water

Peel, quarter, and core the apples. Cut into thin slices lengthwise. Place in a saucepan with water, sugar, and optional lemon juice. Cover and simmer on low heat until apples are tender, about 5 min.

Mix potato flour and water. Away from the heat, stir in the thickening. Bring back to the boil. Set aside to cool. Serve with milk.

Variation: *Gooseberry Compote*   *Krusbärskräm*

Replace the apples with 600 ml (good pint / 2½ cups) half-ripe, topped and tailed gooseberries. Use 85 g (3 oz / scant ½ cup) sugar. Omit the lemon juice. Proceed as described above.

Variation: *Soft Fruit Compote*   *Kräm med bär*

Replace the apples with 300–400 ml (½–⅔ pt / 1¼–1⅔ cups) fresh or frozen berries, eg. raspberries, strawberries, or blueberries. Omit the lemon juice. Proceed as described above.

Gooseberry Compote and Cherry Compote made with fresh berries.

Swiss Meringue   8 servings

Marängsviss

For the meringues—24 shells
2 egg whites
170 g/6 oz/good ¾ cup caster sugar

Whisk the egg whites to stiff peaks with sugar.
Put the meringue in blobs on a buttered and floured baking sheet.
Bake in a 100°C/212°F oven for about 45 min.
Leave the shells to dry in the oven, for instance overnight.

Chocolate Sauce:
40 g/1½ oz/scant ½ cup cocoa powder
85 g/3 oz/scant ½ cup sugar
50 ml/1¾ fl oz/scant ¼ cup each water
   and cream

Place all the ingredients in a saucepan. Blend well. Bring to the boil, and set aside to cool. Instead of water and cream, 100 ml/(3½ fl oz/scant ½ cup) water may be used. The sauce will then get a good strong chocolate flavour.

To assemble:
24 meringue shells
chocolate sauce
300 ml/½ pt/1¼ cups whipping cream

Whip the cream. Arrange meringue shells and cream in alternate layers in a serving bowl. Trickle over the chocolate sauce. Serve chilled.

Angel's Food   4 servings

Änglamat

300 ml/½ pt/1¼ cups whipping cream
2–4 rusks or 15–20 small fancy rusks or
   biscuits
200 ml/7 fl oz/good ¾ cup lingonberry
   jam or cranberry sauce

Whip the cream.
Crumble the rusks.
Mix whipped cream, rusks, and lingonberry jam. Arrange in individual bowls or in a serving bowl.
Serve chilled.

Cones with Fruit and Cream   20 cones

Strutar med bärgrädde

150 g/5⅓ oz/⅔ cup butter
125 g/4½ oz/⅔ cup sugar
150 g/5⅓ oz/good cup flour
3 egg whites

Filling:
300 ml/½ pt/1¼ cups whipping cream
50–100 ml/1¾–3½ fl oz/¼–scant ½ cup
   cloudberry or lingonberry jam

Cream butter and sugar until light and fluffy. Blend in the flour. Whisk the egg whites to stiff peaks and fold them gently into the mixture.
Mark circles, appr. 12 cm (5 in) diameter, on a buttered and floured baking sheet.
Spread the paste thinly within the circles.
Bake in a 175°C/350°F oven for 5–7 min.
While still warm, loosen the cakes with a sharp knife. Shape into cones. If some of the last cakes get stiff before they are shaped, you may soften them by returning the baking-sheet to the oven for a minute or two.
Whip the cream. Fold in the jam.
Fill the cold cones with the cream mixture.

Variation: *Rolled Wafers*   *Rullrån*
Follow the recipe above but make the cakes only 8 cm diameter.
Shape into cylinders.
Serve with jam and whipped cream.

Vanilla Cream Sauce (uncooked) 4–6 servings   *Rårörd vaniljsås*

2 eggs
2 tbs icing (confectionary) sugar
1 tbs vanilline sugar or 2 tsp vanilla extract
300 ml / ½ pt / 1 ¼ cups whipping cream

Beat eggs, icing sugar, and vanilline sugar until light and fluffy, using an electric beater.
Whip the cream. Fold the cream (and the vanilla extract, if used) into the egg mixture.

Vanilla Cream Sauce 4–6 servings   *Vaniljsås*

2 egg yolks
1–2 tbs sugar
200 ml / 7 fl oz / good ¾ cup whipping cream
100 ml / 3 ½ fl oz / scant ½ cup milk
piece of vanilla bean
100 ml / 3 ½ fl oz / scant ½ cup whipping cream

Mix egg yolks, sugar, 200 ml of the cream, milk, and vanilla bean in a saucepan. Place on very low heat and stir continously until the sauce thickens. Use a wooden fork or spatula in an aluminium saucepan to prevent the sauce from discolouring. Leave the sauce to cool, stirring from time to time.
Whip 100 ml cream. Remove the vanilla bean from the sauce and fold in the cream.

Custard Sauce 4–6 servings   *Vaniljsås med vanillinsocker*

2 egg yolks
200 ml / 7 fl oz / good ¾ cup each milk and whipping cream
1 tbs sugar
2 tsp potato flour
1 tbs vanilline sugar or 2 tsp vanilla extract

Mix egg yolks, milk, cream (or milk only), sugar, and potato flour in a saucepan. Place on very low heat and stir continuously until the sauce thickens.
Leave to cool. Beat in the vanilline sugar or the vanilla extract.

Homemade Ice Cream 4 servings   *Hemgjord glass*

60 g / 2 oz / ½ cup raisins
3 tbs Swedish Punch or 2 tbs arrack + 1 tbs water (or 3 tbs dark rhum)
75–100 g / 2 ½–3 ½ oz plain chocolate
2 egg yolks
1 tbs icing (confectionary) sugar
300 ml / ½ pt / 1 ¼ cups whipping cream

Macerate the raisins in the punch, arrack or rhum for a few hours. Chop the chocolate coarsely.
Beat the egg yolks with the sugar until the mixture thickens. Whip the cream. Fold egg mixture, chocolate, raisins and punch into the cream. Turn into a mould or bowl, about 1 l (1¾ pt / 4¼ cups).
Place in the deep-freeze and leave until set, at least 4 hours. Take out the mould about 30 min. before serving.
Unmould the ice cream on to a serving platter or spoon into individual bowls or glasses.

The Swedish Bread

The daily bread has always been important, both practically and symbolically. It had to be satisfying and to keep well. In the old days rye was the grain most readily available, and so rye bread was most commonly baked.

The interest for homemade bread in now increasing steadily. The best bread is that baked in the old way—with coarsely ground, scalded flour or with leaven, but with less sugar and fat than before. Some people even try to bake crisp bread (the most Swedish of them all). It can be baked in an ordinary oven, but it does, of course, get very hard.

All the breads in this chapter can easily be baked at home. Fresh yeast is specified in the recipes, but dried yeast of the fermipan type may be used just as well. Follow the directions on the packet.

Bread is now mostly baked from wheat and rye flour, but oats and barley flour are also used and sometimes a mixture of three or four grains. Traditionally the bread was sweetened with treacle (molasses), but nowadays many types of unsweetened bread are available. Swedish crisp bread is now internationally known and can be bought in many countries. The flat bread is delicious, but less well-known outside Sweden. It can be made at home with excellent result (see recipes on page 88).

In Sweden bread is rarely eaten plain with meals as is the custom abroad. Instead it is made into open sandwiches, smörgåsar. They are eaten with coffee in the morning, as a quick lunch or snack, with soup, or whenever you feel hungry. Swedish sandwiches are usually not very elaborately made, just a slice of bread and butter and a slice of cheese, sausage, ham, or boiled eggs.

Rye Bread   5 round cakes

Skräddakakor

50 g/1¾ oz fresh yeast or corresponding quantity of instant dried yeast, eg. Harvest Gold
50 g/1¾ oz/scant ¼ cup butter
500 ml/18 fl oz/good 2 cups milk
50 ml/1¾ fl oz/scant ¼ cup treacle (molasses)
2 tsp salt
2 tsp crushed aniseed
2 tsp crushed fennel seed
about 825 g/1¾ lb sifted rye flour (a mixed flour, containing 60 % wheat and 40 % rye)

Crumble the yeast in a bowl.
Melt the butter in a saucepan. Pour in the milk. Warm the milk to 37°C/98°F (blood heat). Pour the milk on to the yeast. Stir until the yeast is dissolved. Add treacle, salt, aniseed, fennel seed, and most of the flour. Mix to a dough and knead well. Cover and leave to rise for about 30 min.
Turn out the dough on to a floured pastry board. Knead until smooth and pliable. Add more flour as required.
Divide the dough into 5 parts. Form each one into a smooth round ball.
Roll them out into round cakes, about 2 cm (¾ in) thick.
Place on buttered or baking paper-lined baking sheets.
Make a hole in the middle of each cake, using a scone cutter or a small glass. Prick the cakes all over with a fork. Cover and leave to prove until they look light and porous, about 30 min.
Bake in a 250°C/480°F oven until browned and baked through, about 10 min.
Place on a rack and cover with a cloth. Leave to cool.

Set Soured Milk.

Coarse Rye Bread 2 loaves

*50 g/1¾ oz fresh yeast or corresponding
quantity of instant dried yeast, eg.
Harvest Gold
25 g/1 oz butter
500 ml/18 fl oz/good 2 cups water
2 tsp salt
50 ml/1¾ fl oz/scant ¼ cup treacle
(molasses) or sugar
2 tsp crushed caraway seeds, aniseed, or
fennel seeds (optional)
about 660 g/1½ lb coarsely ground
bread flour of wheat and rye*

*or
350 g/¾ lb coarsely ground rye flour
and 240–300 g/8½–10½ oz/2½–3½
cups plain white bread flour*

Crumble the yeast in a basin.
Melt the butter in a saucepan. Add the water and warm to 37°C/98°F (blood heat).
Pour the mixture on to the yeast. Stir until the yeast is dissolved. Add salt, treacle or sugar, and optional spices.
Mix in most of the flour and knead well.
Cover and leave to rise for about 30 min.
Turn out the dough on to a floured pastry board. Knead until smooth and elastic. Add more flour as required.
Divide the dough into two equal parts and form them into loaves.
Place on a buttered or baking paper-lined baking sheet.
Slash the loaves with a razor blade or a sharp knife. Cover and leave to prove until they look light and porous, about 30 min.
Bake in a 175°C/350°F oven until browned and baked through, about 40 min.
Wrap the loaves in a cloth and leave to cool.

Scalded Rye Bread 2 large loaves

*1l/1¾ pts/4¼ cups boiling water
750 g/1⅔ lb coarsely ground rye flour
100 g/3½ oz fresh yeast or corresponding quantity of instant dried
yeast, eg. Harvest Gold
150 ml/5½ fl oz/⅔ cup fermented milk
or buttermilk
1 tbs salt
50 ml/1¾ fl oz/scant ¼ cup treacle
(molasses)
about 600 g/1 ⅓ lb plain white bread
flour*

Put the rye flour in a bowl. Pour in the boiling water. Mix well. Cover with a cloth and leave overnight or for 2–3 hours, until cool.
Add the yeast dissolved in fermented milk (if you use instant dried yeast, mix it with the white flour), salt, and treacle. Knead in white flour until the dough is firm. Cover and leave to rise for about 30 min. Turn out on to a floured work surface and knead until the dough is smooth and pliable.
Divide into two equal parts. Form 2 large round loaves. Place on a buttered or baking paper-lined baking sheet. Slash the top of the dough with a razor blade or with a sharp knife.
Cover and leave to rise until they look light and porous, about 40 min.
Bake in a 175°C/350°F oven until the loaves are browned and baked through, about 1½ hours. Wrap in a cloth and leave to cool.

*Crisp Flatbread, Rye Bread, Coarse Rye Bread, Scalded Rye Bread, Loaves
with Orange Peel, Country Style Bread with Leaven and Pan Loaves.*

Country Style Bread with Leaven   4 loaves

Lantbröd med surdeg

Leaven:
50 g/1¾ oz fresh yeast or corresponding
  quantity instant dried yeast, eg.
  Harvest Gold.
300 ml/½ pt/1¼ cups tepid water, appr.
  37°C/98°F
165 g/scant 6 oz/1¼ cups sifted rye flour
  (60 % wheat, 40 % rye)
– – –
700 ml/1¼ pts/3 cups tepid water, appr.
  37°C/98°F
30 g/1 oz lard or butter (at room
  temperature)
1 tbs salt
good 1.1 kg/2½ lb sifted rye flour

Crumble the yeast in a basin. Add the water and stir until the yeast is dissolved. Blend in the flour. Cover and leave in room temperature for 24 hours.

Second day: Pour the water into a mixing bowl. Add butter or lard, salt, most of the flour, and the leaven. Knead well. The dough should be pliable but rather firm. Cover and leave to rise for about 1 hour. Turn out on to a floured work surface. Knead until the dough is elastic. Divide into 4 pieces. Form into round loaves. Place on a buttered or baking paperlined baking sheet. Slash the top of the loaves with a razor blade or a sharp knife. Cover and leave to prove until the loaves look light and porous, 30–40 min.

Bake in a 200°C/400°F oven until the loaves are browned and baked through, about 40 min.

Loaves with Orange Peel   3 loaves

Pomeranslimpor

50 g/1¾ oz fresh yeast or corresponding
  quantity of instant dried yeast, eg.
  Harvest Gold
500 ml/18 fl oz/good 2 cups tepid milk,
  appr. 37°C/98°F
75 g/2⅔ oz lard or butter
  (at room temperature)
50 ml/1¾ fl oz/scant ¼ cup treacle
  (molasses)
1 tsp salt
4 tbs ground dry orange peel
550 g/20 oz sifted rye flour (60 % wheat,
  40 % rye)
about 360 g/13 oz white plain flour

Crumble the yeast in a mixing bowl. Pour on the milk and stir until the yeast is dissolved.

Add lard or butter, treacle, salt, orange peel, sifted rye flour, and most of the white flour. Mix into a dough. Cover and leave to rise for about 30 min.

Turn out on to a floured work surface and knead until the dough is smooth and pliable. Add more flour as required. Divide the dough into 3 parts. Form into 25–30 cm (10–12 in) long 'sausages' and place them close together in a buttered roasting pan or on a baking paper in a roasting pan.

Brush with oil or melted butter between the loaves to make it easier to separate them when baked.

Leave to rise until they look light and porous, about 30 min. Bake in a 200°C/400°F oven until browned and baked through, about 40 min.

Place the loaves on a rack and cover them with a cloth. Leave to cool.

Pan Loaves 2 loaves

*50 g/1¾ oz fresh yeast or corresponding
quantity instant dried yeast, eg. Harvest Gold
500 ml/18 fl oz/good 2 cups tepid
water, appr. 37°C/98°F
50 g/1¾ oz lard or butter (at room temperature)
1 tbs salt
720 g/good 1½ lb strong plain flour*

Crumble the yeast in a mixing bowl. Pour in the water. Stir to dissolve the yeast.

Add lard or butter, salt, and most of the flour. Knead into an elastic dough.

Cover and leave to rise for about 30 min.

Turn out on to a floured work surface. Knead until smooth and pliable. Cut the dough into 2 pieces. Form into loaves. Place in buttered 1.5 l (2¾ pts/6½ cups) bread tins. Cover and leave to prove until the loaves look light and porous, about 30 min. Bake in a 200°C/400°F oven until browned and baked through, about 40 min.

Turn out on to a rack, cover with a cloth, and leave to cool.

Steamed Rye Bread from Uppland 1 loaf

*100 g/3½ oz fresh yeast or corre-
sponding quantity of instant dried
yeast, eg. Harvest Gold
700 ml/1⅓ pts/3 cups tepid water,
about 37°C/98°F
1 tsp salt
100 ml/3½ fl oz/scant ½ cup treacle
(molasses)
750 g/1⅔ lb/6⅓ cups rye flour
about 900 g/2 lb/6⅓ cups plain white
flour*

Crumble the yeast in a mixing bowl. Pour on the water. Stir to dissolve the yeast.

Add salt, treacle, rye flour, and most of the plain flour. Mix to an elastic dough. Roll into cylinder shape. Place the loaf in an upright position in a buttered and floured, round and tall mould, for instance a large tin with 15 cm (6 in) diameter.

Cover and leave to rise until doubled in bulk, about 3 hours.

Cover the tin with aluminium foil and place it in a saucepan with simmering water. The water should reach ⅔ up the sides of the tin. Steam for 3 hours. Turn the loaf out and put it back into the tin upside down. Cover and steam until cooked through, appr. another 2 hours.

Turn out and leave to cool, wrapped in a cloth.

Cut the loaf into 4 parts lengthwise before slicing it.

Soft Flatbread · 8–10 rounds

about 10 g/⅓ oz fresh yeast or corresponding quantity instant dried yeast, eg. Harvest Gold
500 ml/18 fl oz/good 2 cups milk
50 ml/1¾ fl oz/scant ¼ cup treacle (molasses)
1 tsp salt
½ tsp ammonium carbonate
220 g/½ lb/1⅔ cups sifted rye flour (60 % wheat, 40 % rye)
100 g/3½ oz/good ¾ cup barley flour
360–480 g/12–16 oz/2½–3½ cups plain white flour

Crumble the yeast in a mixing bowl. Warm the milk until tepid, about 37°C/98°F.

Pour the milk on to the yeast and stir to dissolve. Blend in treacle, salt, and ammonium carbonate. Add sifted rye flour, barley flour, and about 300 g (10 oz/1¼ cups) of the plain flour. Knead until the dough is elastic and rather soft. Leave to rise for 1–2 hours.

Heat an unbuttered baking sheet in a 250°C/480°F oven.

Turn out the dough on to a well-floured work surface. Knead until smooth and pliable. Form into a long sausage. Cut into 8–10 pieces. Roll out each piece to a large thin circle. Sprinkle the work surface rather heavily with flour. Prick with a fork. Bake the flatbreads as they get ready on the hot baking sheet in the oven until lightly browned, 3–4 min.

Fold the cakes and leave to cool wrapped in cloths. Place in plastic bags before they get completely cold.

If you prefer a crisp flatbread, then bake a little longer and leave the breads to cool uncovered, on a rack.

Crisp Flatbread · 24 rounds

15 g/½ oz fresh yeast or corresponding quantity instant dried yeast, eg. Harvest Gold
500 ml/18 fl oz/good 2 cups tepid water, about 37°C/98°F
2 tsp salt
600 g/1⅓ lb/5 cups 4-grain bread flour (mixed from wheat, rye, barley, and oats)

To roll out:
about 180 g/6 oz/1¼ cups plain white flour

Crumble the yeast in a mixing bowl. Pour on the water. Stir to dissolve the yeast.

Add salt and bread flour. Knead to an elastic dough.

Turn out the dough on to a floured work surface. Cut into 3 parts. Form each part into a sausage and cut it into 8 pieces. Form each piece into a round ball. Cover and let rise for about 30 min.

Roll out each ball into a very thin circle. N.B. Do not knead!

Roll and turn the cake several times. When it is very thin, about 2 mm (1/12 in), prick very closely with a fork. Make a hole in the middle of each cake. Place two cakes on each baking sheet. Bake at once in a 275°C/525°F oven for 3–4 min.

Cool on a rack.

Coffee party with seven kinds of cakes

Coffee is the Swedish national drink above all. Traditionally it was served at any time of the day and the kettle was usually kept hot in Swedish homes.

Nowadays coffee vending machines and automatic coffee percolators are found at every place of work and many Swedes drink coffee morning, midday, afternoon, and evening. It is, however, comparatively rare to take part in a coffee party with the traditional seven kinds of cakes.

The fine sweet buns and cakes and the elaborate fancy cakes are now eaten less, but oldfashioned rusks and biscuits may provide wholesome snacks.

The coffee party with the many delicious cakes is, however, part of the Swedish food tradition. Many Swedes allow themselves such a treat on special occasions, for instance to celebrate a name-day on a real summer day during the "Lady's Week" in the end of July. In the old days you sampled all the different kinds, but you did not need to finish them. Whatever you could not eat, you brought home. This tradition is still observed in some places.

What makes the Swedish baking tradition particularly attractive is its variety. There is something for everybody, for every mood and occasion. Only a few of the more well-known recipes can be given here.

The ingredients are well-known. Plain flour and baking powder are always used as self-raising flour is not used in Sweden. Some recipes call for ammonium carbonate. If this is not available, substitute double quantity of baking powder. The final result will, however, be less crisp. Unless otherwise specified use granulated sugar, which is equivalent to the Swedish *strösocker*.

Almond Cuts 20 cakes   *Mandelkubbar*

100 g/3½ oz/scant ½ cup butter
125 g/4½ oz/⅔ cup sugar
1 egg
10 ground bitter almonds or
  10 drops of bitter almond essence
330–360 g/11½–12¾ oz/2–2½ cups
  plain white flour
2 tsp baking powder or 1 tsp ammonium
  carbonate
150 ml/¼ pt/⅔ cup soured cream

To decorate:
50–100 ml/1¾–3½ fl oz/¼–½ cup
  crushed lump sugar

Cream butter and sugar until light. Add the egg, almonds or almond essence, and the flour, mixed with baking powder or ammonium carbonate.

Blend in the soured cream. The mixture should be rather soft. Turn out the dough on to a floured pastry board. Form into a sausage, about 40 cm (16 in) long. Cut into 20 pieces.

Dip the cut surface into crushed lump sugar. Place the cakes on a buttered or baking paper-lined baking sheet.

Bake in a 200°C/400°F oven for 10–15 min.

Cool on a wire rack.

Whole Wheat Rusks   about 100 rusks   *Grahamsskorpor*

50 g/1¾ oz fresh yeast or corresponding
    quantity of instant dried yeast, eg.
    Harvest Gold
200 g/7 oz/scant cup butter or
    150 g/good 5 oz lard
500 ml/18 fl oz/good 2 cups milk
45–85 g/1½–3 oz/¼-scant ½ cup sugar
½ tsp salt
240 g/8½ oz/scant 1¾ cups whole
    wheat flour
about 480 g/good pound/scant 3½ cups
    plain white flour

For the kneading:
60 g/2 oz/scant ½ cup plain white flour
1 tsp ammonium carbonate

Crumble the yeast in a mixing bowl. Melt butter or lard in a saucepan. Add milk and warm until tepid, about 37°C/98°F.

Pour on to the yeast and stir to dissolve.

Add sugar, whole wheat flour and plain flour. Knead until the dough is soft and pliable. Cover and leave to rise until doubled in bulk, 30–40 min.

Sift the additional flour with the ammonium carbonate on to your work surface. Turn out the risen dough.

Knead in the flour and continue kneading until the dough is elastic.

Divide the dough into 5 pieces. Form into long sausages. Put on to buttered or baking paper-lined baking sheets. Brush the sides with melted butter to prevent them from sticking together.

Cover and leave to prove until they look light and puffy, about 40 min.

Bake in a 225°C/435°F oven for about 15 min. Place on a wire rack and cover with a cloth. Leave to cool.

Cut the loaves into 3 cm (1¼ in) slices and halve each slice lengthwise. Arrange on baking sheets.

Put the rusks in a 225°C/435°F oven to colour for about 5 min., then leave them to dry in the residual heat, leaving the oven door open.

Variation: *Spiced Rusks*   *Kryddskorpor*
Follow the master recipe. You may omit the whole wheat flour and use plain flour only (720 g/1 lb 10 oz/5 cups). Add 1 tbs ground bitter orange peel or 2 tsp crushed cardamom. Proceed as described above.

Almond Rusks   about 45 small rusks   *Mandelskorpor*

100 g/3½ oz almonds
100 g/3½ oz/scant ½ cup butter
85 g/3 oz/scant ½ cup sugar
2 eggs
210 g/7½ oz/1½ cups plain white flour
1 tsp baking powder

Blanch and skin the almonds. Chop them coarsely. Cream butter and sugar until light and fluffy. Add the eggs, one at a time, the almonds, and the flour, sifted with the baking powder. Mix quickly to a dough.

Divide the dough into 3 pieces and form each piece into a long sausage. Place on a buttered or baking paper-lined baking sheet.

Bake in a 225°C/435°F oven for 10–12 min. Leave on the baking sheet to cool a little. Cut on the bias into 2 cm (¾ in) pieces. Dry in a 100°C/212°F oven for about 20 min.

Farmhouse Cookies about 30 cookies

Bonnakringlor

*440 g/1 lb/3⅓ cups sifted rye flour (60 %
  wheat, 40 % rye) or 480 g/1 lb
  1 oz/3⅓ cups plain white flour
2 tbs sugar
½ tsp salt
3 tsp ammonium carbonate
100 g/3½ oz lard
300 ml/½ pt/1¼ cups soured cream*

Mix flour, sugar, salt, and ammonium carbonate together on your work surface.

Cut the lard in slices and put them on top of the flour mixture. Cut and then rub the lard into the flour until the mixture is crumbly.

Make a well in the centre, add the soured cream, and mix with your hands to a firm dough.

Form the dough into a sausage. Divide into 30 pieces. Form each piece into a finger-thick sausage. Turn into pretzel shape or form an oval. Place on a buttered or baking paper-lined baking sheet.

Bake in a 250°C/480°F oven for about 8 min. Cool on a wire rack.

These Farmhouse Cookies are made according to a recipe from Småland. The cookies may be brushed with beaten egg and dipped in crushed lump sugar.

Potato Cookies   about 40 cookies

*2 medium-sized cold boiled potatoes
(appr. 200 ml/7 fl oz/good ¾ cup
grated potatoes)
125 g/4½ oz/good ½ cup butter at room
temperature
3 grated bitter almonds
180 g/6⅓ oz/1¼ cups plain white flour*

To decorate:
*about 100 ml/3½ fl oz/scant
½ cup crushed lump sugar*

Grate the potatoes. Take care not to pack them together if you are going to measure them.
Cream the butter. Blend in the potatoes, bitter almonds, and flour.
Turn out the dough on to your work surface and knead until smooth. Shape into long thin sausages. Divide into pieces, about 20 cm (8 in) long. Turn into pretzel shape. Dip the topside into crushed lump sugar.
Place on a buttered or baking paper-lined baking sheet.
Bake in a 200°C/400°F oven for about 15 min.
Cool on a wire rack.

Butter Cookies   about 30 cookies

*210 g/7½ oz/1½ cups plain white flour
200 g/7 oz/good ¾ cup butter
50 ml/1¾ fl oz/scant ¼ cup soured
cream*

To decorate:
*1 egg
about 100 ml/3½ fl oz/scant
½ cup crushed lump sugar*

Put the flour on your work surface. Cut the butter in slices and put them on top of the flour. Cut and then rub the butter into the flour until you have a crumby mixture. Add the soured cream and mix quickly with your hands to form a dough. Chill for about 30 min.
On the floured work surface roll out the dough evenly ½–1 cm (¼–⅓ in) thick. With a knife or a pastry wheel cut the pastry into strips, 1 cm (scant ½ in) wide and 20 cm (8 in) long. Turn into pretzel shape.
Brush with beaten egg and dip into crushed lump sugar.
Place on an unbuttered baking sheet.
Bake in a 250°C/480°CF oven for about 5 min.
Cool on a wire rack.

Crisp Cookies   about 40 cookies

*150 g/5¼ oz/⅔ cup butter
65 g/2⅓ oz/⅓ cup sugar
200 ml/7 fl oz/good ¾ cup soured
cream
300–360 g/10½–12½ oz/2–2½ cups
plain white flour
2 tsp ammonium carbonate*

To decorate:
*1 egg
about 100 ml/3½ fl oz/scant ½ cup
crushed lump sugar*

Cream butter and sugar until light and fluffy. Add the soured cream. Sift the flour with the ammonium carbonate and blend it into the mixture. Mix to a dough. Form into very thin sausages. Cut into pieces about 20 cm (8 in) long. Turn into pretzel shape. Brush with beaten egg and dip into crushed lump sugar.
Place on a buttered or baking paper-lined baking sheet.
Bake in a 225°C/435°F oven for about 8 min.
Cool on a wire rack.

Coffee Bread   about 50 buns or 4 lengths   *Vetebröd*

*50 g/1¾ oz fresh yeast or corresponding
    quantity instant dried yeast, eg.
    Harvest Gold*
100–150 g/3½–5¼ oz/½–⅔ cup butter
500 ml/18 fl oz/good 2 cups milk
85 g/3 oz/scant ½ cup sugar
½ tsp salt
1 egg
2 tsp ground cardamom (optional)
*about 900 g/2 lb/6⅓ cups plain white
    flour*

Filling:
*50 g/1¾ oz/scant ¼ cup butter, at room
    temperature*
45 g/1½ oz/scant ¼ cup sugar
*1 tbs ground cinnamon, cardamom, or
    vanilline sugar*

To glaze:
1 egg
crushed lump sugar (optional)

Crumble the yeast in a mixing bowl. Melt the butter in a saucepan. Pour in the milk and warm until tepid, about 37°C/98°F. Pour the liquid over the yeast and stir to dissolve. Add sugar, salt, egg, and optional cardamom. Blend in most of the flour and knead until the dough is pliable but not too firm. Cover and leave to rise for about 30 min.

Turn out the dough on to a floured work surface and knead until springy and elastic. Divide the dough into 4 pieces. Roll out each piece into a rectangle, about 20 × 30 cm (8 × 12 in). Spread with butter and sprinkle with sugar and cinnamon, cardamom, or vanilline sugar.

Roll up the dough lengthwise like a jelly roll, finishing with the seam downwards.

Buns: Cut the roll into 3 cm (1¼ in) pieces. Place cut surface upwards in paper cases or on a paper-lined baking sheet.

Lengths: Place the dough rolls on a baking paper-lined baking sheet. With scissors, cut slanting gashes about 2 cm (¾ in) apart. Lift and turn the resulting flaps alternately to the right and to the left to form a petal design.

Cover and leave to prove until puffy and light, about 30 min. Brush with beaten egg and sprinkle with crushed lump sugar (optional).

Bake buns in a 250°C/480°F oven for 8–10 min. and lengths at 200°C/400°F for about 20 min.

Put on a wire rack and cover with a cloth. Leave to cool.

Saffron Buns (Christmas Buns)   about 45 small buns   *Saffransbröd*

*50 g/1¾ oz fresh yeast or corresponding
    quantity instant dried yeast, eg.
    Harvest Gold*
200 g/7 oz/scant cup butter
500 ml/18 fl oz/good 2 cups milk
½–1g saffron
85–130 g/3–4½ oz/½–⅔ cup sugar
½ tsp salt
*about 780 g/1¾ lb/5½ cups plain white
    flour*
60 g/good 2 oz/scant ½ cup raisins

To glaze:
1 egg

Crumble the yeast in a mixing bowl. Melt the butter in a saucepan. Pour in the milk and warm until tepid, about 37°C/98°F. Pour the liquid over the yeast and stir to dissolve. Add saffron, sugar, salt, and most of the flour. Knead until smooth and pliable, but not too firm.

Cover and leave to rise for 30–40 min.

Turn out on to a floured work surface and knead until elastic.

Form into finger-thick sausages. Cut into pieces and shape each piece into the letter S. Place the buns on buttered or baking paper-lined baking sheets.

Press on a few raisins as decoration. Cover and leave to prove until they look light and puffy, about 30 min.

Brush with beaten egg.

Bake in a 225–250°C/435–480°F oven for 8–10 min.

Place on a wire rack and cover with a cloth. Leave to cool.

This dough can be used for other Christmas breads as well.

Lenten Buns   12 buns

25 g/1 oz fresh yeast or corresponding quantity instant dried yeast, eg. Golden Harvest
50 g/1¾ oz/scant ¼ cup butter
200 ml/7 fl oz/good ¾ cup milk
¼ tsp salt
45 g/1½ oz/scant ¼ cup sugar
1 egg
360–420 g/12½–14½ oz/2½–3 cups plain white flour

To glaze:
1 egg

Fillings:
● *crumb from the buns*
75 g/2¾ oz almond paste
50 ml/1¾ fl oz/scant ¼ cup milk or cream
200 ml/7 fl oz/good ¾ cup whipping cream
icing sugar (optional)

● *crumb from the buns*
50 g/1¾ oz almonds
45 g/1½ oz/scant ¼ cup sugar
75 ml/2⅔ fl oz/⅓ cup milk or cream
200 ml/7 fl oz/good ¾ cup whipping cream
icing (confectionary) sugar (optional)

To serve:
hot milk

These buns, traditionally eaten on Shrove Tuesday, are now so popular that they start to appear in the confectioner's shops immediately after Christmas. Try them—they are delicious.

Crumble the yeast in a mixing bowl. Melt the butter in a saucepan. Pour in the milk and warm until tepid, about 37°C/98°F. Pour over the yeast and stir to dissolve. Blend in salt, sugar, egg, and most of the flour. Knead until the dough is smooth and pliable. Cover and leave to rise for about 30 min.
Turn out the dough on to a floured pastry board and knead until it is springy and elastic. Cut the dough into 2 pieces. Form each into a sausage and divide into 6 pieces. Form into round smooth rolls. Place the rolls on a buttered or baking paper-lined baking sheet. Cover and leave to prove until they look light and puffy, 30–40 min.
Brush with beaten egg.
Bake in a 250°C/480°F oven for 8–10 min. Put the buns on a wire rack and cover with a cloth. Leave to cool.
Cut the top off each bun. Scoop out some of the crumb. Mash with a fork.
Filling I: Grate the almond paste. Mix crumb, almond paste, and milk or cream.
Filling II: Grind the almonds. Mix crumb, almonds, sugar, and milk or cream.
Fill the buns with one of the almond mixtures. Whip the cream. Pipe or spoon the cream on to the buns. Put the tops back on.
Dust the tops with optional icing sugar.
The buns may be served with hot milk, but they are excellent with coffee.

Brown Cuts   about 70 cookies

200 g/7 oz/scant cup butter
130 g/4½ oz/⅔ cup sugar
50 ml/1¾ fl oz/scant ¼ cup treacle (molasses)
1 egg
3 tsp ground cinnamon
2 tsp ground cardamom
360 g/12⅔ oz/2⅓ cups plain white flour
2 tsp baking powder

Cream butter, sugar, and treacle until light and fluffy. Blend in egg and spices. Sift the flour with the baking powder. Add it to the butter mixture and blend to a paste. Divide into 5 parts. Form into long sausages.
Place the sausages on a buttered or baking paper-lined baking sheet. Flatten them a little.
Bake in a 200°C/400°F oven for about 15 min. Cool. Cut diagonally into 2 cm (¾ in) pieces.

Gingerbread Cookies   150–200 cookies

Pepparkakor

255 g/9 oz/1¼ cups sugar
150 ml/¼ pt/⅔ cup treacle (molasses)
200 g/7 oz/scant cup butter
150 ml/¼ pt/⅔ cup whipping cream
1 tbs ground ginger
1 tbs ground cinnamon
½ tbs ground cloves
1 tbs bicarbonate of soda
about 720 g/1 lb 9 oz/5 cups plain
    white flour

Place sugar, treacle, and butter in a saucepan. Heat until melted.

Pour the mixture into a mixing bowl and allow to cool a little. Stir in cream and spices.

Mix the bicarbonate with a little of the flour and stir it into the mixture.

Blend in the rest of the flour, but keep some back for moulding. Work the dough well. Leave to rest overnight.

Roll out the dough very thinly on a floured pastry board and cut into different shapes with pastry cutters.

Place the biscuits on buttered or baking paper-lined baking sheets. Bake in a 200°C/400°F oven for about 5 min.

Cool a little and remove from the baking sheet.

Saffron Buns, Gingerbread Cookies, Fried Waffles and Crullers.

Almond Shells   40–45 shells

Mandelmusslor

100 g/3½ oz almonds
200 g/7 oz/scant cup butter
85 g/3 oz/scant ½ cup sugar
1 egg
210 g/7½ oz/1½ cups plain white flour

Blanch, skin, and grind the almonds. Cream butter and sugar until light and fluffy.
Blend in egg and almonds. Add the flour and mix to a dough. Chill for 30 min.
Form the dough into a sausage and divide into 40–45 even pieces.
Press the dough down into small fluted pastry moulds.
Bake in a 200°C/400°F oven for 10–12 min.
Unmould and leave to cool.

Jam Cuts   about 40 cookies

Skurna syltkakor

Short Crust Pastry:
270 g/9½ oz/scant 2 cups plain white
   flour
65 g/2¼ oz/⅓ cup sugar
200 g/7 oz/scant cup butter

To decorate:
100 ml/3½ fl oz/scant ½ cup jam
90 g/3¼ oz/⅔ cup icing (confectionary)
   sugar
1 tbs water

Place flour and sugar on the pastry board. Cut the butter into slices and put it on top of the flour. Cut and then rub the butter into the flour until you have a crumbly mixture. Mix with your hands to a dough.
Divide the dough into 5 parts. Form each part into a sausage, about 2 cm (¾ in) diameter. Place on a buttered or baking paper-lined baking sheet. With your finger press down along the middle of the dough, making a shallow groove.
Put a little jam in the groove.
Bake in a 175°C/350°F oven for about 15 min.
Mix icing sugar and water to a smooth paste. Spread thinly over the lengths while still warm and cut at once diagonally into 3 cm (1¼ in) pieces.

Rye Biscuits   about 50 biscuits

Kavlade rågkakor

165 g/5¾ oz/1¼ cups sifted rye flour
   (60 % wheat, 40 % rye)
60 g/2 oz/scant ½ cup plain white flour
45 g/1½ oz/scant ¼ cup sugar
150 g/5⅓ oz/⅔ cup butter
1 egg

Place flour and sugar on your work surface. Cut the butter into slices and put it on top of the flour. Cut and then rub the butter into the flour until the mixture is crumbly. Add the egg. Mix with your hands to a dough. Set aside to rest for about 30 min.
Roll out thinly. Prick the dough with a fork. Cut into rounds with a pastry cutter. Make a little hole, using for instance an apple corer, near the edge of each biscuit. Put the biscuits on a buttered or baking paper-lined baking sheet.
Bake in a 200°C/400°F oven for about 5 min. Cool a little, and remove from the baking sheet.

Cardamom Cake

75 g/2⅔ oz/⅓ cup butter
170 g/6 oz/good ¾ cup sugar
2 eggs
180 g/6⅓ oz/1¼ cups plain white flour
1½ tsp baking powder
2 tsp ground cardamom
150 ml/¼ pt/⅔ cup soured cream

Cream butter and sugar together until light and fluffy. Add the eggs, one at a time. Mix flour, baking powder, and cardamom. Fold in the flour mixture and the soured cream alternately. Turn the mixture into a buttered and floured 1.5 l (3 pts/6½ cups) tin.
Bake in a 175°C/350°F oven for about 1 hour.
Unmould the cake and leave to cool.

Sunshine Cake

150 g/5⅓ oz/⅔ cup butter
3 eggs
170 g/6 oz/good ¾ cup sugar
150 g/5⅓ oz/good cup plain white flour
1 tsp baking powder
about 15 almonds or half of a 35 g-pac-
  ket of almond flakes

Melt the butter and set aside to cool. Beat eggs and sugar until light and fluffy.
Add the butter. Mix flour and baking powder and fold it into the mixture.
Turn into a buttered and floured 2 l (3½ pts/8½ cups) tin.
Bake in a 175°C/350°F oven for about 10 min. Meanwhile, blanch, skin, and flake the almonds. Sprinkle them on to the cake and continue baking for another 30–35 min.
Leave the cake in the tin for some minutes.
Turn out, but reverse the cake immediately so its almond side is uppermost. Leave to cool.

Swedish Almond Cake

100 g/3½ oz/scant ½ cup butter
215 g/7½ oz/good cup sugar
4 egg yolks
200 g/7 oz cold boiled potatoes (about
  3 medium-sized potatoes)
150 g/5⅓ oz almonds
grated rind of ½ lemon (well scrubbed)
4 egg whites

To decorate:
icing (confectionary) sugar

Lemon sauce:
2 egg yolks
2 tbs icing (confectionary) sugar
200 ml/7 fl oz/good ¾ cup whipping
  cream
juice of ½ lemon

Mash or rice the potatoes. Grind the almonds.
Cream butter and sugar until light and fluffy. Blend in the egg yolks, one at a time.
Fold in potatoes, almonds, and lemon rind.
Beat the egg whites until stiff and fold them gently into the mixture.
Turn into a buttered and floured tin with removable base, capacity 2 l (3½ pts/8½ cups).
Bake in a 175°C/350°F oven for 40–50 min. Allow to cool a little and then remove the mould. Dust with icing sugar when the cake is cool.
Serve with lemon sauce or whipped cream, flavoured with grated lemon rind.
Cream egg yolks and sugar until light and fluffy. Whip the cream and fold it into the egg-mixture.
Flavour with lemon juice.

Swiss Roll (Jelly Roll) about 10 pieces *Bärrulltårta*

3 eggs
130 g/4½ oz/⅔ cup sugar
60 g/2 oz/⅓ cup potato flour or corn starch
1 tsp baking powder

Filling:
300 ml/½ pt/1¼ cups whipping cream
500 ml/18 fl oz/good 2 cups fresh strawberries or 1 packet frozen straw-berries, about 225 g/8 oz

Beat eggs and sugar together until light and fluffy. Mix potato flour or corn starch and baking powder.
Fold it into the egg-mixture. Pour on to a baking paper-lined rectangular tin, about 30 × 40 cm (12 × 16 in).
Bake in a 250°C/480°F oven for about 5 min. Sprinkle a little sugar on the cake.
Turn out on to a greaseproof paper. Brush the baking paper with a little water if you have difficulties loosening it from the cake. Remove the paper. Leave the cake to cool.
Whip the cream and spread it over the cake. Rinse and slice fresh strawberries or thaw frozen ones. Distribute the berries over the cake.
Roll up the cake gently around the filling.
Serve chilled.

Fried Waffles about 40 waffles *Struvor*

2 eggs
2 tbs sugar
100 ml/3½ fl oz/scant ½ cup cream
100 ml/3½ fl oz/scant ½ cup milk
120 g/4½ oz/good ¾ cup plain white flour

To deep-fry:
lard, coconut butter, or oil

To decorate:
granulated sugar

Beat the eggs with the sugar. Add cream and milk alternately with the flour. Stir until the batter is smooth. Leave to rest for 15 min.
Heat the fat (at least 5 cm/2 in deep) in a heavy saucepan. Test the temperature by frying a piece of white bread. If the bread turns golden in 1 min., the temperature is correct, 175–180°C/350–356°F.
Heat the waffle iron in the fat for a few moments. Then dip it gently into the batter, but not too far—the batter must not come over the top. Lower the iron gently into the hot fat and fry until the waffle is nicely golden, about 1 min. Detach it from the iron and set it to drain on kitchen paper. Repeat the procedure with the next waffle.
When the waffles are done, dip them in granulated sugar. Store in an airtight tin.

For these waffles you need a different kind of waffle iron from that used for the Crisp Waffles on page 73. It consists of a fancy shape of cast iron — some are star-shaped, others shaped like butterflies, etc. — on the end of a long handle.

Coffee Bread, a Swedish Almond Cake and several Swedish Cookies.

Crullers about 50

50 g/1¾ oz/scant ¼ cup butter
5 yolks
45 g/1½ oz/scant ¼ cup sugar
grated rind of ½ lemon (well scrubbed)
1 tbs brandy
210 g/7½ oz/1½ cups plain white flour

To deep-fry:
lard, coconut butter, or oil

To decorate:
granulated sugar

Melt the butter and allow to cool. Cream the egg yolks with the sugar for a couple of minutes, not too long or blisters will form in the crullers. Add butter, lemon rind, and brandy.

Blend in the flour and mix to a dough. Turn out on to your pastry board and knead until elastic, but not too firm. Leave to rest for about 30 min.

Roll out thinly. With a pastry wheel cut the dough into rectangular pieces, about 3 × 10 cm (1¼ × 4 in), and cut a lengthwise slit in the middle of each piece. Slip one end of the dough through the slit and turn it inside out.

Heat the fat (at least 5 cm/2 in deep) in a heavy saucepan.

Test the temperature by frying a piece of white bread. If the bread turns golden in 1 min. the temperature is right, 175–180°C/350–356°F.

Place a few crullers at a time in the pan. Fry until golden brown on both sides.

Remove the crullers with a slotted spoon. Set on kitchen paper to drain.

Turn them in granulated sugar.

Illustrations:
Susanne Gunnarsson

Pickles and preserves

The ability to preserve foods and store them for future needs was important in the old days. Among the methods used were preservation by means of sugar, salt, or vinegar. With modern cold storage and an ample supply of fresh food the year round, there is no longer any need to "bottle" vegetables and fruit. Many Swedes still do it, mostly because of the "home made" taste, but maybe for the sake of tradition too. It gives a nice and cozy feeling to have jars filled with cucumbers, pots with beetroots and apple sauce, and why not some bottles of lingonberry drink.

An advantage with homebottling is that one has full control over the sugar content and the addition of preservatives.

In this chapter you will find the recipes for many of the sweet-and-sour accompaniments, which will give an authentic Swedish touch to your meal. Start with something really easy, for instance the Swedish Cucumber Salad, and you will be tempted to go on.

Pickled Cucumbers

Ättiksgurkor

1 kg/2¼ lbs small green cucumbers, 7–10 cm/3–7 in
10 heads of dill
1 piece of fresh horseradish

For the pickle:
400 ml/14 fl oz/1⅔ cups 12 % essence of vinegar or American regular white vinegar
600 ml/good pint/2½ cups water
or:
800 ml/scant 1½ pts/3⅓ cups cider or white wine vinegar
200 ml/7 fl oz/good ¾ cup water

255 g/9 oz/good cup sugar
2 tbs salt
1 piece of mace
or 1 tbs yellow mustard seeds
10 white peppercorns

Scrub the cucumbers clean in cold water. Rinse the dill heads.

Peel and dice the horseradish.

Place the cucumbers, dill heads, and horseradish in alternate layers in a jar or pot.

Mix all the ingredients for the pickle in a saucepan. Bring to the boil and skim.

Pour the hot pickle over the cucumbers. Cover and leave in a cool place for 3 days.

Pour off the pickle and bring it to the boil. Pour the hot pickle over the cucumbers.

Put a weight on top of the cucumbers to keep them in the pickle.

Store in a dark and cool place. The cucumbers may be eaten after a month, but they keep considerably longer.

Variation:
Follow the master recipe, but slice the cucumbers. Instead of the second boiling of the pickle, add ¼ tsp sodium benzoate, dissolved in a little pickle. The sliced cucumbers may be eaten already after 1–2 weeks.

Gherkins

Saltgurkor

2 kg/4½ lbs small green cucumbers
8–10 blackcurrant leaves
10 heads of dill
1 piece of horseradish
10 white peppercorns
1 piece of dried ginger

For the pickle:
1 l/1¾ pts/4¼ cups water
100 ml/3½ fl oz/scant ½ cup 12 %
    essence of vinegar or American
    regular white vinegar
or:
900 ml/good 1½ pts/3¾ cups water
200 ml/7 fl oz/good ¾ cup cider or
    white wine vinegar

125 g/scant 4½ oz/scant ½ cup salt,
    preferably without iodine
¼ tsp sodium benzoate

Boil the pickle first of all: Mix water, vinegar, and salt in a saucepan. Bring to the boil. Add sodium benzoate. Leave to cool.

Scrub the cucumbers clean in cold water. Rinse blackcurrant leaves and dill heads.

Peel and dice the horseradish.

Arrange cucumbers, blackcurrant leaves, dill heads, horseradish, and spices in alternate layers in a jar or pot—top and bottom layers should be blackcurrant leaves and dill heads. Pour the pickle over the cucumbers. Put a weight on top of them to keep them in the pickle.

Store in a dark and cool place. They may be eaten after 3–4 weeks.

Sweet Pickled Pumpkin

Syltad pumpa

2 kg/4½ lbs European pumpkins
water
2 tsp salt per litre/1¾ pts/4¼ cups water

For the pickle:
200 ml/7 fl oz/good ¾ cup 12 %
    essence of vinegar or American
    regular white vinegar
300 ml/good ½ pt/1¼ cups water
or:
400 ml/14 fl oz/1⅔ cups cider or white
    wine vinegar
100 ml/3½ fl oz/scant ½ cup water

340 g/12 oz/1⅔ cups sugar
2 pieces mace
2 pieces dried ginger
5 white peppercorns
1 tsp yellow mustard seeds

Peel the pumpkins. Cut them in halves. Remove the seeds. Cut into pieces the size of a lump of sugar.

Boil the pumpkins in lightly salted water until just tender, about 5 min. Remove the pumpkins and drain.

Pickle: Mix vinegar, water, and sugar in a saucepan. Tie up the spices in a piece of gauze or cheesecloth and put the packet in the saucepan.

Bring to the boil and skim.

Drop in the pumpkin pieces, a few at a time, and boil until tender and transparent, about 15 min. Remove and drain. Place the pumpkins in clean jars or pots.

Boil the pickle uncovered on high heat for about 20 min.

Skim. Leave to cool. Remove the packet of spices and keep it for later use.

Pour the pickle over the pumpkins. Cover.

After a few days, pour off the pickle and boil it again with the spices.

Skim the pickle. Allow it to cool. Pour over the pumpkins. This may be repeated once or twice with a few days' intervals.

The pickle will then become more concentrated and give the pumpkins a stronger flavour.

Store the pumpkins in a dark and cool place. Serve as an accompaniment to meat dishes.

Pickled Beetroots, Pickled Cucumber and Cucumber Salad.

Pickled Beetroots

Inlagda rödbetor

1 kg/2¼ lbs small fresh beetroots
water
1 piece of horseradish

For the pickle:
200 ml/7 fl oz/good ¾ cup 12 %
    essence of vinegar or American
    regular white vinegar
300 ml/½ pt/1¼ cups water
or:
400 ml/14 fl oz/1⅔ cups cider or white
    wine vinegar
100 ml/3½ fl oz/scant ½ cup water

1 tsp salt
170 g/6 oz/good ¾ cup sugar
5 white peppercorns
5 cloves

Cut off the tops about 2 cm (¾ in) from the beetroots. Wash carefully in cold water without damaging the skin. Leave the tips of the roots on. Place the beetroots in boiling water in a saucepan. Cover and boil on low heat until tender, 20–30 min. Remove the beetroots and peel them. If they are big, slice them, otherwise leave them whole. Put them in pots or jars.

Peel and dice the horseradish. Add the diced horseradish to the beetroots.

Mix vinegar, water, salt, sugar, and spices in a saucepan. Bring the pickle to the boil and pour it over the beetroots. Cover and leave to cool. Store in a dark and cool place.

Pickled Onions

Syltlök

1 kg/2¼ lbs pickling onions
water
185 g/6½ oz/⅔ cup salt per litre/1¾
    pts/4¼ cups water

For the pickle:
200 ml/7 fl oz/good ¾ cup 12 %
    essence of vinegar or American
    regular white vinegar
300 ml/½ pt/1¼ cups water
or:
400 ml/14 fl oz/1⅔ cups cider or white
    wine vinegar
100 ml/3½ fl oz/scant ½ cup water

85–170 g/3–6 oz/½–good ¾ cup sugar
5 pieces mace
3 pieces dried ginger
1 tsp white peppercorns

Place the pickling onions in boiling water in a saucepan. Boil for 2 min. Drain and pour on cold water. Peel the onions.

Mix water and salt. Leave the onions in the brine for some hours. Pour off the brine. Boil the onions once more in unsalted water for about 5 min.

Drain the onions and put them in clean glass jars. Tie up the spices in a piece of gauze or cheesecloth.

Pickle: Mix vinegar, water, sugar, and spices in a saucepan. Bring to the boil. Remove the packet of spices and keep it for later use. Skim the pickle.

Pour the pickle over the onions.

After 24 hours, pour off the pickle and boil it down with the spices. Remove the spices, skim the pickle, and leave to cool. Pour it over the onions and cover the jars. Store in a dark and cool place.

Cucumber Salad

300 g/10 oz fresh cucumber

Dressing:
2 tbs 12 % essence of vinegar or
American regular white vinegar
100 ml/3½ fl oz/scant ½ cup water
or:
4 tbs cider or white wine vinegar
70 ml/2½ fl oz/scant ⅓ cup water

2 tbs sugar
⅛ tsp white pepper
¼ tsp salt
2 tbs chopped parsley

Rinse the cucumber. Slice it thinly. Put the slices in a bowl. Dressing: Mix vinegar, water, sugar, salt, and pepper. Pour the dressing over the cucumber. Sprinkle with parsley. Chill for a couple of hours.

Apple Sauce

3 kg/6½ lbs apples, preferably of a tart
and firm kind
500 ml/18 fl oz/good 2 cups water
765 g/1 lb 11 oz/3¾ cups sugar
juice of 1 lemon
½ tsp sodium benzoate

Rinse and peel the apples. Quarter and core. Place them in a saucepan. Add the water. Cover and simmer on low heat until the fruit is tender but not quite mushy, about 15 min. Stir from time to time to prevent the fruit from sticking to the pan.
Away from the heat, blend in the sugar. Bring to the boil.
Blend in the lemon juice and the sodium benzoate mixed with a little purée. Put the apple purée in clean, warmed pots. Cover and leave to cool. Store in a dark and cool place.

Variation: *Sieved Apple Purée*   *Passerat äppelmos*
Quarter the apples, but do not peel or core. Boil the apple quarters for about 10 min. Force through a strainer. Otherwise as described above.

Ginger Pears

1 kg/2¼ lbs small firm pears
500 ml/18 fl oz/good 2 cups water
510 g/1 lb 2 oz/2½ cups sugar
3 pieces dried root ginger
⅛ tsp sodium benzoate

Peel the pears, but leave the stalks on. Scrape the stalks with a knife and cut a cross at the top of the pears.
Mix water, sugar, and ginger in a saucepan. Bring to the boil.
Drop in a few pears at the time. Boil until tender, about 10 min.
Remove the pears and put them in clean, warmed glass jars. Boil down the syrup uncovered on high heat.
Mix the sodium benzoate with a little of the syrup and add it to the saucepan.
Pour the syrup over the pears. Cover the jars.
Leave to cool. Store in a dark and cool place.

Pears with Lingonberries

about 600 g/1⅓ lb lingonberries
300 ml/½ pt/1¼ cups water
510–680 g/1 lb 2 oz–1½ lb/
2½–3⅓ cups sugar
1 kg/2¼ lb small firm pears

Pick over the lingonberries and rinse them. Put them in a saucepan. Add water and sugar. Bring to the boil and simmer uncovered on low heat for about 10 min.

Meanwhile peel the pears, but leave the stalks on. Scrape the stalks with a knife and cut a cross at the top end of the pears. Put the pears in the saucepan and let them boil with the lingonberries until the pears are tender, about 10 min. Skim well. Put the fruit in clean, warmed pots. Pour over the syrup.

Cover the pots and leave to cool. Store in a dark and cool place.

Lingonberry Jam (cooked)

about 1 kg/2¼ lb lingonberries
510–680 g/1 lb 2 oz–1½ lb/2½–3⅓
cups sugar
300 ml/½ pt/1¼ cups water

Pick over the berries and rinse them. Alternate the berries with sugar in a saucepan. Add water and bring to the boil. Simmer uncovered on low heat for 15–20 min. Shake the saucepan, so that the berries get evenly heated.

Remove from the heat. Skim.

Put the jam in cleaned, warmed pots. Cover and leave to cool.

Store in a dark and cool place.

Variation: *Lingonberry Jam with Spices*   *Lingonsylt med kryddor*
Cook the jam as described in the master recipe, but use only 340 g (12 oz/1 ⅔ cups) sugar and 100 ml (3½ fl oz/ scant ½ cup) water. Add 1 cinnamon stick, 5 cloves, and the shredded rind of 1 lemon (well scrubbed).

Raw Lingonberry Jam

about 1 kg/2¼ lb lingonberries
510–680 g/1 lb 2 oz–1½ lb/2½–3⅓
cups sugar

Pick over the berries and rinse them. Put them in a large mixing bowl. Add sugar, a little at a time, and stir with a wooden fork or spatula until the sugar is dissolved and the berries mushy. You may also use an electric mixing machine to prepare this jam.

Put the jam in clean cold pots. Cover.

Store in a dark and cool place or freeze.

Ginger Pears and Pears with Lingon-
berries are oldfashioned and delicious
ways of bottling pears.

Cloudberry Jam

1 kg/2¼ lb cloudberries
340–510 g/12–18 oz/1⅔–2½ cups
* sugar*

Cloudberries grow on the swamps in Northern Sweden. They are used fresh or frozen for desserts or made into jam or *mylta*. Ice cream with hot cloudberries is a well-known Swedish delicacy.

Pick over the berries and rinse if necessary.
Place the berries in layers with the sugar in a saucepan. Let stand for a while to release the juice.
Bring to the boil and simmer, uncovered, on low heat for 10–15 min.
Shake the saucepan from time to time, so that the berries are evenly heated.
Skim. Put the jam in clean, warmed pots. Cover.
Leave to cool. Store in a dark and cool place.

Variation: *Mylta*
Fill bottles or pots with clean, dry cloudberries. Shake to pack them together. There should be as little air as possible left in the bottle or pot. Close with screw caps or corks. Store in a dark and cool place.

Lingonberry Drink

about 1 kg/2¼ lb lingonberries
500 ml/18 fl oz/good 2 cups water
1 tsp citric acid
255–340 g/9–12 oz/1¼–1⅔ cups sugar

Pick over the berries and rinse them. Drain well.
Mash the berries in a basin, using for instance a potato masher.
Pour in the water. Add citric acid. Stir. Cover the basin.
Let stand in a cool place for 1–2 days. Stir from time to time. Turn into a muslin bag and let the juice run through for about 30 min. Mix juice and sugar, stirring until the sugar dissolves. Skim. Pour into clean, cold bottles. Close with screw caps or corks. Store in a dark and cool place.

Lingonberry Drink and various kinds of Lingonberry Jam. Cranberry sauce makes an excellent substitute for lingonberry jam.

Softfruit Syrup (cooked)

about 1 kg/2¼ lb soft fruit, raspberries, strawberries, cherries, red or black currants
water—300 ml/½ pt/1¼ cups for raspberries
—400 ml/14 fl oz/1⅔ cups for cherries
—500 ml/18 fl oz/good 2 cups for red currants
—700 ml/1¼ pt/3 cups for black currants
425–510 g/15–18 oz/2–2½ cups sugar per litre/1¾ pts/4¼ cups juice
¼ tsp sodium benzoate

Fruit syrup is very popular in Sweden. Diluted with water it makes a refreshing drink, particularly in summer time. Slightly thickened with potato flour it makes a sauce to be served with desserts like rice pudding or semolina pudding. If more potato flour is used, it turns into a jelly-like cream which is a very popular dessert served with milk or light cream.

Pick over the berries and rinse them. Bring the water to the boil in a saucepan. Add the berries. Cover and simmer on low heat for about 10 min. Press the berries against the side of the saucepan to extract the juice.
Strain the juice through a muslin bag (without squeezing) for about 30 min.
Rinse the saucepan. Measure the juice and pour it into the saucepan. Add the sugar.
Bring the syrup to the boil. Skim.
Stir in the sodium benzoate, mixed with a little of the syrup. Pour the syrup into clean, warmed bottles. Close with screw caps or corks. Leave to cool. Store in a dark and cool place.

Soft Fruit Jam (cooked)

about 1 kg/2¼ lb soft fruit, eg. raspberries, strawberries, or bilberries/blueberries
425 g/15 oz/good 2 cups sugar (340 g/12 oz/1⅔ cups for bilberries)
¼ tsp sodium benzoate

Pick over the berries and rinse them. Drain well.
Place the berries in a saucepan. Slowly bring to the boil.
Cover and simmer on low heat for about 5 min.
Blend in the sugar. Simmer uncovered on low heat for about 15 min. Skim.
Stir in the sodium benzoate, mixed with a little of the jam.
Turn the jam into clean, warmed pots. Cover and leave to cool. Store in a dark and cool place.

Variation: *Gooseberry Jam* *Krusbärssylt*
Top and tail the berries. Boil with 100 ml (3½ fl oz/scant ½ cup) water for 15–20 min. Proceed as described above.

Variation: *Cherry Jam* *Körsbärssylt*
Stone the cherries. Crush some of the stones and add the kernels to the cherries. Add 100 ml (3½ fl oz/scant ½ cup) water and boil for 10 min. Proceed as described above.

Variation: *Black Currant Jam* *Svart vinbärssylt*
Strip the black currants from their stalks. Boil with 300 ml (½ pt/1¼ cups) water for about 5 min. Proceed as described above.

Black Currant Jelly

Svart vinbärsgelé

about 1 kg/2¼ lb ripe black currants
400 ml/14 fl oz/1⅔ cups water
680 g/1½ lb sugar per litre/1¾ pt/4¼
cups juice

Rinse the black currants. There is no need to remove the stalks.
Drain.
Bring the water to the boil in a saucepan. Add the berries. Cover and simmer on low heat for about 10 min. Press the berries against the saucepan to extract the juice.
Turn into a muslin bag and let the juice drip through without pressure for about 30 min. Rinse the saucepan. Measure the juice and pour it into the pot. Boil uncovered for about 5 min. Blend in the sugar. Let the syrup boil for 5–20 min. without stirring. Test the jelly by dipping a spoon in the syrup. Then lift the spoon high above the pot. When the drops are heavy, the jelly is ready.
Remove the pot from the heat. Leave to stand for a few minutes. Skim. Turn into clean, warmed pots. Leave to cool. Pour on a thin layer of paraffin wax. Cover. Store in a dark and cool place.

Variation: *Red Currant Jelly*   *Röd vinbärsgelé*
Cook the jelly as described in the master recipe, but use only 300 ml (½ pt/1¼ cups) water.

Variation: *Rowan Jelly*   *Rönnbärsgelé*
Substitute frost-bitten rowan berries (berries of mountain ash), mixed with sliced apples (optional) for the currants. Use 500 ml (18 fl oz/good 2 cups) water. Proceed as described in the master recipe.

Rose Hip Purée

Nyponmos

about 1 kg/2¼ lb fresh rose hips
300–500 ml/10–18 fl oz/1¼–2 cups
water
sugar to taste

Pick over the rose hips and rinse them. Boil in the water until tender, about 1 hour. Use less water if the fruit is going to be puréed in an electric mixing machine, more if it is going to be rubbed through a sieve.
Purée the rose hips while still warm in an electric mixer or rub them through a sieve.
Sweeten to taste.
This purée has to be frozen, if it is to be stored.

Festive Food

Feasts used to mean a lot as longed-for breaks in the daily toil. There were many reasons for feasts. Family celebrations such as birthdays, christenings, confirmations, banns, weddings, and even funerals. Harvest and parish meetings also gave occasion for festive gatherings.

It was important to find time to be together, to see one's family, neighbours, and friends and together enjoy the festive food, so very different from the monotonous daily fare.

Feast dishes were all those things, which were too expensive or too rare to be eaten regularly. The dishes served were numerous and varied, because everybody brought food along; thus it became a kind of surprise party.

Large feasts are no longer common. Both the number of guests and the number of dishes have been reduced. Anyone who can prepare some tasty dishes suitable for cooking on a larger scale, such as a festive fish gratin or an oldfashioned pot roast, can entertain without trouble. This has helped to keep the traditional Swedish hospitality alive.

The Cold Table   SMÖRGÅSBORD

Originally the *smörgåsbord* was intended as an hors d'oeuvre, a great number of different dishes (most of them cold, but some hot), served with bread and butter and accompanied with beer and snaps. The modern variety, served in many Swedish restaurants, is a complete meal, including some hot dishes and a simple dessert.

A large-scale *smörgåsbord* is rarely served in private homes nowadays. Most families have, however, a few special favourites, which may be served as a first course.

The recipes in this chapter are all suitable, if you want to make your own *smörgås-bord*. Choose one or two herring dishes plus the Smoked Herring Salad, a couple of the hot dishes, and a selection of cold meats, a paté, and one or two kinds of cheese. Pickled beetroots, gherkins, lingonberry jam, and mustard should accompany the cold meats, and don't forget the boiled potatoes, the soured cream, and chives for the pickled herring. Add a selection of breads (eg. a white bread, a rye bread, and some crisp bread) and some butter and your *smörgåsbord* is ready.

Pickled Salt Herring

*2 large salt herring fillets or 1 tin desalted
    pickling herrings, appr. 420 g/15 oz*

For the pickle:
*75 ml/2⅔ fl oz/⅓ cup 12 % essence of
    vinegar or American regular white
    vinegar*
150 ml/¼ pt/⅔ cup water
or:
*150 ml/¼ pt/⅔ cup cider or white wine
    vinegar*
75 ml/2⅔ fl oz/⅓ cup water

85–125 g/3–4⅓ oz/½–⅔ cup sugar
10 crushed allspice berries
3 cloves
1 bay leaf
1 red onion or 2–3 shallots
1 piece of leek

Soak the fillets in plenty of cold water for 12 hours or over-night. Rinse the pickling herrings under running cold water.
Pickle: Mix vinegar, water, sugar, and spices in a saucepan.
Bring to the boil and set aside to cool.
Peel and slice the onion or the shallots. Rinse the leek and cut it into fine strips.
Cut the herring fillets into pieces, appr. 2 cm (¾ in) wide.
Alternate the pieces with layers of onion and leek in a pot or small jar. Pour in the pickel with the spices. Refrigerate for at least 24 hours before serving.

Variation: *Herring with Juniper Berries*   *Enbärssill*
Omit cloves and bay leaf and use instead 15 dried juniper berries. Crush the juniper berries and distribute them be-tween the layers of herring and onion/leek in the jar.
Sprinkle with chopped dill. Proceed as described above.

The Glaziers' Herring

2 salted herrings

For the pickle:
*100 ml/3½ fl oz/scant ½ cup 12 %
    essence of vinegar or American regu-
    lar white vinegar*
150 ml/¼ pt/⅔ cup water
or:
*200 ml/7 fl oz/good ¾ cup cider or
    white wine vinegar*
50 ml/1¾ fl oz/scant ¼ cup water

65–85 g/2¼–3 oz/⅓–½ cup sugar
15 white peppercorns
10 allspice berries
2 bay leaves

1 red onion or 2–3 shallots
1 small carrot
1 piece horseradish

Clean the herrings, but leave skin and backbones. Soak the herrings in plenty of cold water for 24 hours.
Pickle: Mix vinegar, water, sugar, and spices in a saucepan.
Bring to the boil and set aside to cool.
Peel the vegetables. Slice onion and carrot, dice the horse-radish.
Cut the herrings into 2 cm (¾ in) pieces across the back-bone.
Arrange herrings, onion, carrot, and horseradish in alter-nate layers in a pot or a small jar.
Pour in the pickle with the spices.
Refrigerate for at least 24 hours before serving.

The Swedish smörgåsbord is made of several groups of dishes to be eaten in a certain order. There are varieties of pickled salt herring, smoked or poached fish, cold cuts and salads, hot dishes, and cheese. Start with the pickled herring accompanied by a boiled potato and some soured cream. Return to the table for a clean plate and a selection from the next group of dishes. Colour illustration on following page.

Mustard-marinated Herrings

Senapsgravad strömming

1 kg/2¼ lb Baltic herrings, Smelts or 600 g/1⅓ lb herring fillets

Pickle:
100 ml/3½ fl oz/scant ½ cup 12 % essence of vinegar or American regular white vinegar
500 ml/18 fl oz/good 2 cups water
or:
200 ml/7 fl oz/good ¾ cup cider or white wine vinegar
400 ml/14 fl oz/1⅔ cups water

Mustard Sauce:
100 ml/3½ fl oz/scant ½ cup prepared mustard
½ tbs salt
2 tbs sugar
2 tbs vinegar
50 ml/1¾ fl oz/scant ¼ cup water
100 ml/3½ fl oz/scant ½ cup cooking oil
50 ml/3 rounded tbs chopped dill or chives

Clean and rinse the herrings. Remove backbone and skin.
Pickle: Mix vinegar and water in a bowl. Place the herring fillets in the pickle and leave to marinate for about 4 hours.
Mix mustard, salt, sugar, vinegar, and water. Blend in the oil.
Add dill or chives.
Drain the herring fillets carefully.
Alternate them with layers of sauce in a pot or a serving bowl.
Refrigerate for 24 hours before serving.
The herrings will keep for about a week.

Spiced Baltic Herring

Kryddströmming

0.75 kg/1⅔ lb Baltic herrings or smelts

Pickle:
150 ml/¼ pt/⅔ cup 12 % essence of vinegar or American regular white vineger
350 ml/good 12 fl oz/1½ cups water
or:
300 ml/½ pt/1¼ cups cider or white wine vinegar
200 ml/7 fl oz/good ¾ cup water

Spice mixture:
2 tbs coarse salt
3 tbs sugar
2 tsp allspice berries
2 tsp white peppercorns
1 tsp cloves
2 bay leaves
2 pieces mace
1 onion

Clean and rinse the herrings, but leave the backbone. Put the herrings in a pot or jar.
Mix vinegar and water. Pour it on to the herrings, so that they are completely covered. Cover and leave in a cool place for 24 hours.
Drain the herrings carefully.
Spice mixture: Mix salt, sugar, and spices in a mortar. Crush and mix all together. Peel and slice the onion.
Arrange the herrings, the spice mixture, and the onion slices in alternate layers in the pot or jar.
Cover and leave in a cool place or refrigerate for about 1 week before serving.
The herrings will then keep for 1–2 weeks.

Herrings with Eggs and Green Herbs

Sillfat med ägg och grönt

2 large or 4 smaller de-salted salt herring fillets
½ leek
3–4 hard-boiled eggs
50 ml/3 rounded tbs finely chopped dill
50 g/1¾ oz/scant ¼ cup butter

Cut the herring fillets in pieces and arrange them on a serving dish. Rinse the leek and cut it into fine strips. Peel and chop the eggs. Sprinkle leek, eggs, and dill over the herrings. Heat the butter until it is lightly browned. Pour it hot over the herrings just before serving. Serve with boiled new potatoes.

Smoked Herring Salad

Böcklingsallad

4 smoked herrings
2 medium-sized apples
4 pickled beetroots
iceberg lettuce or Chinese cabbage

Sour Cream Sauce:
200 ml/7 fl oz/good ¾ cup soured
   cream
½–1 tbs grated horseradish
50 ml/3 rounded tbs chopped dill
¼ tsp salt
¼ tsp white or black pepper

Clean and fillet the smoked herrings. Rinse, core, and dice the apples. Chop the beetroots. Rinse and shred the lettuce or Chinese cabbage. Arrange the ingredients in separate rows or heaps on a serving dish.

Mix soured cream, horseradish, and dill. Season the sauce with salt and pepper.

Hand the sauce separately.

Poached Mackerel 4 servings

Inkokt makrill

1 kg/2¼ lb mackerel

Court bouillon:
1 l/1¾ pt/4¼ cups water
1 tbs salt
1–2 bay leaves
5 white peppercorns
5 allspice berries
a few sprigs of dill
2 tbs lemon juice

Clean and rinse the fish. Cut it in 4 cm (1½ in) pieces across the backbone.

Court-bouillon: Bring the water to the boil with salt, spices, dill, and lemon juice. Simmer for a few minutes. Put the fish in a wide shallow saucepan. Pour in the court-bouillon. It should just cover the fish. Cover and poach on low heat for 8–10 min. Leave the fish to cool in the stock. Serve with a sauce of soured cream, seasoned with dill, salt, and pepper.

Variation: *Poached Eel* *Inkokt ål*
Follow the master recipe, but skin the eel. Poach for 15–20 min.

Jansson's Temptation 4 servings

Janssons frestelse

2 onions
butter
8 medium-sized potatoes, about
   750 g/1⅔ lb
1 tin (appr. 100 g/3½ oz) filleted
   Swedish anchovies or 2 tins of
   anchovies in oil
300 ml/½ pt/1¼ cups cream
2 tbs breadcrumbs

Outside of Sweden Jansson's Temptation is one of the most wellknown Swedish dishes. It is excellent both at the "hot end" of the *smörgåsbord* and for a week-end lunch. It is easy to prepare, if you cannot get Swedish anchovies, anchovies in oil or salt herring will do.

Peel the onions and slice them thinly. Soften in butter in a frying pan. Peel the potatoes and cut them into matchstick lengths. Butter an ovenproof dish. Put in half the potatoes, then the onions and the anchovies. Cover with the rest of the potatoes. Pour over some of the anchovy liquor or oil (optional), then the cream. Sprinkle with breadcrumbs.

Bake in a 200°C/400°F oven, until the potatoes are tender and the surface is nicely browned, 45–50 min.

Smoked Herring Gratin 4 servings

Böcklinglåda

300 ml/½ pt/1¼ cups milk
1 leek
butter
6–8 smoked herrings
3 eggs
½ tsp salt
¼ tsp white or black pepper

Bring the milk to the boil. Set aside to cool.
Rinse the leek and cut it into fine strips. Soften it in butter in a frying pan.
Clean and fillet the smoked herrings.
Beat eggs and milk together. Season with salt and pepper.
Arrange herrings and leek in alternate layers in a buttered ovenproof dish. Pour on the batter.
Bake in a 200°C/400°F oven, until the batter has set and the top is nicely browned, about 20 min.

Meatballs 4–6 servings

Köttbullar

400 g/14 oz minced meat, eg. beef,
    mixed beef and pork, or veal and
    pork
1 egg
2 tbs potato flour
200 ml/7 fl oz/good ¾ cup milk, cream,
    or water
1 tsp salt
¼ tsp white or black pepper
¼ tsp ground allspice
1 tbs grated raw onion (optional)
butter

This is a small and crisp variety of the main course meatballs. They are used on open sandwiches or served on the *smörgåsbord*.

Mix egg, potato flour, liquid, salt, spices, and optional onion together. Add the minced meat and work until the mixture is smooth.
Dip your hands into cold water and form the mixture into small meatballs (or use 2 spoons).
Put the meatballs on a carving board rinsed with cold water.
Heat a little butter in a frying pan and brown the meatballs, a few at a time. Shake the pan so that they brown evenly. Lower the heat and continue frying until the meatballs are cooked through, about 5 min.
Serve at once, or reheat in a covered pan on the stove or in a 200°C/400°F oven.

Scrambled Eggs 4 servings

Äggröra

6 eggs
150 ml/¼ pt/⅔ cup cream
½ tsp salt
1 tbs butter

Beat eggs, cream, and salt together. Melt the butter in a heavy saucepan. Pour in the egg mixture. Cook on a very low heat, stirring all the time with a wooden fork or a spatula. The eggs are done when they are thick and creamy.
Serve with fried cocktail sausages, smoked reindeer, smoked leg of lamb, or smoked fish.

Stuffed Onions 4—6 servings

4 large onions
water
2 tsp salt per litre/1¾ pts/4¼ cups water

Stuffing:
300 g/10 oz minced meat, veal or lean pork
3 egg yolks
150 ml/¼ pt/⅔ cup cream
1 tsp salt
¼ tsp white pepper
½ tsp crumbled sage (optional)
100 ml/3½ fl oz/scant ½ cup cooking liquid from the onions (optional)

Peel the onions. Blanch them in boiling salted water for about 10 min. Remove the onions, but keep the cooking liquid. Drain the onions and set aside to cool. Blend meat, egg yolks, cream, salt, and spices together. Work until smooth.

Make a slit towards the middle of the onions from the top to the root end. Separate the leaves. Put a little stuffing on each leaf and roll them up, making small packages. Arrange, closely together, in a buttered ovenproof dish.

Bake in a 225°C/435°F oven until browned and cooked through, about 30 min. Baste with a little cooking liquid towards the end of the cooking time (optional).

PARTY SOUPS

Cheese Soup 4 servings

½ leek or 1 onion
2 tbs butter
3 tbs flour
1 l/1¾ pts/4¼ cups stock
200—300 ml/7—10 fl oz/¾—1¼ cups grated cheese
salt and pepper (optional)
1 egg yolk
100 ml/3½ fl oz/scant ½ cup cream

Serving suggestions:
mussles
shelled prawns
diced fresh cucumber
asparagus, cut into pieces
smoked ham, cut into strips

Rinse the leek and cut it into thin strips, or peel and finely chop the onion. Melt the butter in a saucepan. Cook the onion or leek until tender but not browned. Stir in the flour and thin with the stock. Boil for 3—5 min., stirring from time to time. Away from the heat add the cheese and allow it to melt. Season with salt and pepper, if needed. Heat the soup, but do not let it boil.

Beat egg yolk and cream together in the soup tureen. Pour over the hot soup. Serve with one or more of the garnishes suggested above, for instance arranged in small bowls, so that the guests may choose for themselves.

Consommé with Cheese Straws   4 servings   *Klar buljong med oststänger*

*1 l/1¾ pts/4¼ cups clarified brown
    bouillon (see page 34)
1–2 tbs dry sherry (optional)
salt and pepper (optional)*

*Cheese Straws: 15–20 straws
180 g/6⅓ oz/1¼ cups plain flour
200 ml/7 fl oz/good ¾ cup grated
    cheese
150 g/good 5 oz/⅔ cup butter
50 ml/1¾ fl oz/scant ¼ cup soured
    cream*

*To glaze:
beaten egg*

Cheese Straws: Mix flour and cheese on your pastry board. Add the butter, cut and then rub the butter into the flour, until the mixture is crumbly. Add the soured cream and mix quickly to a dough. Chill for 30 min.

Put the dough on the floured pastry board and shape it into 1 cm (½ in) thick sausages. Cut into 10 cm (4 in) pieces. Put them on a buttered or baking paper-lined baking sheet. Brush with beaten egg.

Bake in a 250°C/480°F oven until the cheese straws are golden brown and crisp, 6–8 min.

Heat the bouillon. Season with a little optional sherry and with salt and pepper, if needed.

Serve the consommé with the cheese straws.

Cream of Green Peas   4 servings   *Grön ärtpuré*

*1 small onion
2 packets of frozen green peas, about
    250 g/8 oz each
1 l/1¾ pts/4¼ cups stock
2 tbs butter
2 tbs flour
100 ml/3½ fl oz/scant ½ cup cream
½ tsp salt
¼ tsp white or black pepper*

*Garnish:
150 ml/¼ pt/⅔ cup whipping cream or
    200 ml/7 fl oz/good ¾ cup soured
    cream or crème fraiche
2 tbs grated horseradish
100 g/3½ oz shelled prawns (optional)*

Peel and finely chop the onion. Boil peas and onion in a little of the stock for about 5 min. Purée in a liquidizer or rub through a sieve.

Melt the butter in a saucepan. Blend in the flour and thin with the stock. Add the purée and the cream. Bring to the boil and simmer for about 5 min., stirring from time to time. Season with salt and pepper.

Serve with whipped cream, soured cream, or crème fraiche seasoned with horseradish and with optional prawns.

Cream of Asparagus   4 servings   *Sparrissoppa*

*2 tins of asparagus cuts, 300 g/10 oz each
2 tbs butter
2 tbs flour
1 l/1¾ pts/4¼ cups stock and asparagus
    liquid
salt (optional)
⅛ tsp white or black pepper
2 egg yolks
100 ml/3½ fl oz/scant ½ cup cream*

Drain the asparagus. Melt the butter in a saucepan and blend in the flour. Thin with the stock. Simmer on low heat for 3–5 min. Season with pepper and optional salt. Add the asparagus and heat through.

Beat egg yolks and cream together in the soup tureen. Pour in the hot soup. Serve with cheese straws (see above) or with small cheese canapés.

Consommé with Cheese Straws is an elegant start to a dinner party.

Mushroom Soup   4 servings

Svampsoppa

1–1.5 l/2–2½ pts/4–6 cups fresh, trimmed mushrooms or 2 tins mushrooms, 200 g/7 oz each
or 40–50 g/1½–1¾ oz dried mushrooms, eg. mixed mushrooms, chanterelles, champignons, or morels
2 tbs butter
1 small leek
3 tbs flour
800 ml/scant 1½ pts/3⅓ cups clarified stock and liquid from the tinned mushrooms
300 ml/½ pt/1¼ cups cream
½ tsp salt
¼ tsp black pepper
2–3 tbs sherry or port (optional)

Cut the *fresh* mushrooms into pieces. N.B. if you use morels, they must first be boiled in plenty of water for about 10 min. Discard the cooking liquid.

Drain the *tinned* mushrooms—keep the liquid. Cut the mushrooms into pieces.

Soak the *dried* mushrooms in water for a few hours. Discard the soaking water. Cut the mushrooms into pieces.

Melt the butter in a heavy saucepan. Add the mushrooms and cook until any liquid has evaporated. Rinse the leek and cut it into fine strips. Add it to the mushrooms and cook for a few minutes. Sprinkle the flour on to the mushrooms and stir to mix. Thin with stock, optional mushroom liquid, and cream. Simmer on low heat for 20–30 min, stirring from time to time. Season with salt, pepper, and optional sherry or port.

Serve with bread, butter, and a well-ripened cheese.

Salmon Soup from Halland   4 servings

Halländsk laxsoppa

the head, trimmings, and tail from one small salmon
1 l/1¾ pts/4¼ cups water
1 tsp salt
5 white peppercorns
some sprigs of dill
4 medium-sized potatoes
2 onions
1 piece celeriac (celery-root), appr. 50 g/1¾ oz
200 ml/7 fl oz/good ¾ cup cream
salt and pepper (optional)
50 ml/3 rounded tbs chopped dill

Bring the water to the boil with salt, peppercorns, and dill sprigs in a saucepan. Rinse the fish trimmings and discard the gills. Put the trimmings in the saucepan, cover, and simmer on low heat for about 15 min. Remove the fish. Discard skin and bones from the tail piece. Cut the meat into small pieces. Reserve.

Strain the fish stock and return it to the saucepan.

Peel the potatoes, onions, and celeriac. Cut into small pieces. Add to the fish stock and boil until tender, about 15 min. Rub the vegetables through a sieve or purée them with a little stock in an electric blender.

Return the vegetable purée to the stock. Add the cream and allow the soup to boil, uncovered, for about 5 min.

Season with additional salt and pepper, if needed. Add the reserved fish meat and heat through. Sprinkle with dill.

FISH AND SHELLFISH

Canapés with Whitebait Roe   4 servings

Entrérätt med löjrom

4 slices white bread
1 tbs butter
75–100 g / 2 ½ – 3 ½ oz whitebait roe
  (if you cannot get it, salmon roe will
  serve as a substitute)
1 tbs finely chopped onion
½ lemon
sprigs of dill

Remove the crust from the bread or cut out rounds with a pastry cutter.

Heat the butter in a frying pan. Fry the bread on moderate heat. Distribute the whitebait roe on the bread. Garnish with onion, thin lemon wedges, and small sprigs of dill.

Whitebait Roe can be replaced with other fish roe.

Baked Pike 4 servings

1 pike, about 1.25 kg/2¾ lb
1½ tsp salt
1 egg
2–3 tbs finely sieved white breadcrumbs
about 1 tbs butter
1 small tin filleted Swedish anchovies,
about 50 g/1¾ oz
150 ml/¼ pt/⅔ cup cream

Clean, gill, and scale the fish. Rinse it and drain. Rub with salt. Place the fish, belly down, in a buttered ovenproof dish. Beat the egg. Brush the fish with egg and sprinkle the breadcrumbs evenly over the whole fish. Dot with butter. Bake the fish in a 200°C/400°F oven, for about 20 min. Chop the anchovy fillets and mix them with the cream. Pour the mixture around the fish. Continue cooking until the fish is firm to the touch and nicely browned, 10–15 min. Serve with the stock, boiled potatoes, and a salad. The same recipe may be used for other whole fish, eg. pike-perch, haddock, cod, whitefish, salmon, and large char. Omit the anchovies for whitefish, salmon, and char. The cooking time depends on the thickness of the fish.

Pike Timbale with Shrimp Sauce 4 servings

This fish pudding is similar to the French fish quenelles.

1 pike, about 1 kg/2¼ lb
2 tbs butter, at room temperature
300 ml/½ pt/1¼ cups cream
2 egg yolks
1 tbs flour
2 tsp salt
¼ tsp white pepper
2 egg whites

Shrimp Sauce:
2 tbs butter
1½ tbs flour
300 ml/½ pt/1¼ cups milk and optional
fish stock
100–150 g/3½–5 oz shelled shrimps
(about 300g/10 oz shrimps in their
shells)
100 ml/3½ fl oz/scant ½ cup cream
1 egg yolk
juice and grated peel of ½–1 lemon
½–1 tsp salt
¼ tsp white pepper
chopped dill (optional)

Clean, fillet and skin the fish. Carefully remove all bones. Rinse the fillets quickly and drain. Put the fish twice through the mincer or purée in a blender. Mix in the butter.
Beat cream, egg yolks, flour, salt, and pepper together. Mix it with the fish, for instance using the blender.
Fry a little of the forcemeat in butter in a frying pan and taste it to check the seasoning.
Beat the egg whites until they form stiff peaks. Fold into the forcemeat. Turn into a buttered and floured 1½ l (3 pts/6 cups) mould. Cover the mould with aluminium foil. Place the mould in a tin with enough hot water to come half-way up its sides. Cook in a 200°C/400°F oven for about 1 hour. Meanwhile make the sauce: Melt the butter in a saucepan. Blend in the flour. Thin with milk and optional fish stock, while stirring. Simmer on low heat for 3–5 min. Remove from the heat and stir in the shrimps. Beat cream and egg yolks together and add to the sauce. Heat the sauce, but do not let it boil. Season with lemon peel and juice, salt and pepper. Add the optional dill.
Leave the pike pudding in the mould for a few minutes, then unmould.
Garnish, for instance with shrimps, lemon wedges, and dill. Serve with the sauce, boiled potatoes, and green peas or French beans.

Fresh prawns (shrimps), served with toast, butter, and maybe a good cheese is a simple way to make a party.

Poached Salmon   4 servings

Kokt lax i portionsbitar

4 salmon slices, about 3 cm/1¼ in thick
water
2 tsp salt per litre/1¾ pts/4¼ cups water
5 allspice berries
5 white peppercorns
1 onion
1 carrot
1 bunch dill

Sour-cream Sauce:
200 ml/7 fl oz/good ¾ cup soured
   cream
2 tbs chopped capers
1 tsp prepared mustard, preferably
   unsweetened
50 ml/3 rounded tbs finely chopped dill

Bring the water to the boil in a wide, shallow saucepan. Add salt and spices. Peel the onion and the carrot. Cut them into halves and add them to the court-bouillon, together with the dill. Boil for about 10 min.

Add the fish slices. Cover and poach on low heat until the fish is firm to the touch, 6–8 min. Leave the salmon to cool in its stock.

Mix all the ingredients for the sauce.

Arrange the fish on a serving dish. Serve with boiled potatoes, the sour-cream sauce, and buttered spinach.

Variation: *Salmon, Poached Whole*   *Kokt lax, hel eller i bit*
Poach the salmon as described above, but increase the poaching time to 12–15 min., depending on the thickness of the fish.

Baked Turbot 4 servings

Kokt piggvar

1 turbot, about 1.25 kg/2¾ lb
2 tsp salt

To serve:
melted or browned butter
grated horseradish

Clean, rinse, and dry the fish. Rub with salt. Place in an ovenproof dish.

Cook in a 125°C/255°F oven until the fish is done and the meat around the bone is firm and white, 25–35 min., depending on the thickness of the fish.

Serve the turbot with melted or browned butter, plenty of grated horseradish, and boiled, riced potatoes.

Fish au Gratin with Shellfish 4 servings

Fiskgratäng med skaldjur

500 g/1 lb 2 oz fish fillets, eg. plaice or
sole

Court-bouillon:
400 ml/14 fl oz/1⅔ cups water
1½ tsp salt
5 white peppercorns
a few sprigs of dill

about 100 g/3½ oz shelled shrimps
(250 g/9 oz shrimps in their shells)
1 tin mussels in water, about 225 g/8 oz
50 ml/3 rounded tbs finely chopped dill

Sauce:
2 tbs butter
3 tbs flour
200 ml/7 fl oz/good ¾ cup fish stock
200 ml/7 fl oz/good ¾ cup cream
1 egg yolk
salt
white pepper
50 ml/3 rounded tbs grated cheese

Court-bouillon: Boil the water with salt, pepper, and dill for about 10 min. Fold the fillets in half and place them in a wide, shallow saucepan. Pour in enough court-bouillon so that the fish is barely covered. Cover and poach on low heat for about 7 min.

Place the fish in a buttered ovenproof dish. Arrange shrimps, mussels, and dill on top of the fish. Strain the stock.

Sauce: Melt the butter in a saucepan. Blend in the flour and thin with fish stock and cream. Simmer for 3–5 min. Remove from the heat and stir in the egg yolk. Season with salt and pepper, if needed.

Pour the sauce over fish and shellfish. Sprinkle with cheese. Brown in a 250°C/480°F oven for 10–15 min.

Serve with boiled potatoes, green peas, and a green salad.

Fried Mountain Char 4 servings

Stekt fjällröding eller öring

1–1.25 kg/2¼–2¾ lb char or salmon
trout, 4–6 fishes
2 tsp salt
100 ml/3½ fl oz/scant ½ cup coarsely
chopped dill
2 tbs flour
2 tbs breadcrumbs
½ tsp paprika powder (optional)
2–3 tbs butter

Clean the fish, but leave the heads on. Cut off the fins. Rinse and drain. Sprinkle with salt. Stuff the fish with dill. Mix flour, breadcrumbs, and optional paprika. Coat the fish with this mixture. Brown the butter in a frying pan, arrange the fish in the pan, and fry on rather low heat until done and nicely browned, about 5 min. each side. Serve with boiled potatoes and spinach, cooked whole and seasoned with butter.

Fried Eel 4 servings

1–2 eels, about 1 kg/2¼ lb
2 tsp salt

Coating:
1 egg
3 tbs breadcrumbs
½ leek
1–2 tbs butter
100 ml/3½ fl oz/scant ½ cup finely chopped parsley
100 ml/3½ fl oz/scant ½ cup pickled onions (optional)

Garnish:
lemon wedges

Clean and skin the eels. Cut them into 7–8 cm (3 in) pieces across the backbone. Sprinkle with salt.

Beat the egg. Dip the eel pieces first in egg, then in breadcrumbs.

Rinse the leek and cut it into fine strips.

Heat the butter in a frying pan. Fry the eels on rather low heat until they are nicely browned and cooked through, 5–7 min. each side.

Arrange on a hot serving dish.

Fry leek, parsley, and optional pickled onions in the frying pan. Put this mixture on top of the eel.

Garnish with lemon wedges. Serve with boiled potatoes.

Lobster au Gratin 4 servings

2 boiled lobsters, about 600 g/1⅓ lb

Court-bouillon:
1 tbs butter
200 ml/7 fl oz/good ¾ cup fish stock
100 ml/3½ fl oz/scant ½ cup dry white wine
½ tsp thyme
2–3 white peppercorns

Sauce:
2 tbs butter
1 tbs flour
150 ml/¼ pt/⅔ cup cream
½ tsp salt
⅛ tsp white pepper
1 tsp prepared mustard, preferably unsweetened
2 egg yolks
1 tbs lemon juice

100 ml/3½ fl oz/scant ½ cup grated cheese (well-ripened)

Cut the lobsters in half lengthwise with a heavy knife. Discard the stomach sack, which is found at the very front of each shell-half. Crack the claws with a nut-cracker. Extract the meat and cut it in pieces.

Fry the claw shells in butter in a frying pan. Pour on fish stock and wine. Add thyme and peppercorns. Boil uncovered, on low heat, until about 150 ml (¼ pt/⅔ cup) remains. Strain.

Sauce: Melt the butter in a saucepan. Blend in the flour. Thin with the stock and cream. Boil for 3–5 min. Season with salt, pepper, and mustard. Let the sauce cool a little, then stir in the egg yolk and the lemon juice.

Place the shell halves in an ovenproof dish. Spread a little of the sauce in the shells. Arrange the lobster meat on top.

Pour over the rest of the sauce. Sprinkle with cheese. Bake in a 225°C/435°F oven until the top is nicely browned and all is heated through, about 10 min.

Serve with lemon wedges and dill, toast, butter, and a green salad.

Poached Salmon.

MEAT

Manor-house Roast (a spicy pot roast) 6–8 servings *Slottsstek*

1 kg/2¼ lb boneless beef, for ex. from
  the rump, topround or eyeround
1 onion
1 carrot
butter
1 tsp salt
1 bay leaf
3–4 white peppercorns
3–4 allspice berries
3–4 anchovy fillets (3–4 tbs Chinese soy
  sauce make a good substitute)
1 tbs vinegar
200–300 ml/7–10 fl oz/¾–1¼ cups
  water

Gravy:
500 ml/18 fl oz/good 2 cups liquid
  (braising juices + stock)
3 tbs flour + 50 ml/1¾ fl oz/scant ¼ cup
  water
100 ml/3½ fl oz/scant ½ cup cream
salt, pepper, anchovy liquor (optional)

Tie up the meat with cotton string, if its shape is irregular. Peel and quarter the onion. Scrape the carrot and cut it in pieces. Heat the butter in a roaster or a heavy-bottomed pot and brown the meat all over. Add the onion and let it brown too. Add carrot, salt, bay leaf, peppercorns, anchovy fillets, vinegar, and a little water. Cover and cook on low heat, until the meat is tender, 1¼–1½ hours. Test with a skewer. While cooking, baste with additional liquid if the meat looks dry.

Remove the meat and keep warm.

Gravy: Strain the braising juices into a saucepan. Add stock to make up 500 ml. Bring to the boil. Blend flour and water together. Beat the thickening into the sauce and add the cream.

Boil for 3–5 min.

Season with salt, pepper, and optional anchovy liquor.

Cut the meat into thin slices. Serve with the gravy, boiled vegetables, and for instance redcurrant jelly.

Roast Leg of Pork (Fresh Ham)   6–8 servings   *Skinkstek*

1 kg/2¼ lb rind- and bone-less leg of
  pork
1½ tsp salt
¼ tsp white or black pepper
½ tsp ground ginger

Gravy:
300 ml/½ pt/1¼ cups stock
2 tbs flour + 50 ml/1¾ fl oz/scant ¼ cup
  water
100 ml/3½ fl oz/scant ½ cup cream
salt and pepper
soy sauce (optional)

Rub the meat all around with salt and spices. Place on a rack in a roasting pan. Insert a meat thermometer with its point in the middle of the meat.

Roast in a 175°C/350°F oven until the thermometer shows 85°C/185°F. Allow for approximately 2 hours' roasting time. Deglaze the roasting pan with stock. Strain into a saucepan.

Gravy: Bring the roasting juices to the boil. Mix flour and water. Whisk the thickening into the gravy and add the cream. Boil for 3–5 min. Season with salt, pepper and optional soy sauce.

Cut the meat into thin slices.

Serve with boiled potatoes, the gravy, and boiled vegetables or a salad.

The gravy may be omitted and the roast served with baked potatoes, cooked in the oven at the same time as the meat. Place well-scrubbed potatoes in the oven when appr. 1 hour remains of the roasting time.

Variation: *Roast Veal*   *Kalvstek*

Cook as described in the master recipe, but use 1 kg (2¼ lb) boneless veal, eg. from the fillet or rump. Season with salt and pepper as in the above recipe and also with 1 tsp crumbled rosemary or sage. Roast until the meat thermometer shows 70–72°C/158–162°F if you want the meat to be pink and 77°C/171°F if you want it well done.

Roast Lamb with Herb Butter   8 servings   *Lammstek med kryddsmör*

1 leg of lamb, about 2 kg/4½ lb
2 tsp salt
½ tsp white or black pepper

Herb butter:
- *with dried herbs:*
  50 g/1¾ oz/scant ¼ cup butter
  1 tsp crumbled tarragon
  1 tsp crumbled chervil
  ¼ tsp black pepper
- *with onion and parsley:*
  50 g/1¾ oz/scant ¼ cup butter
  2 tbs onion, chopped very finely
  2 tbs finely chopped parsley

Rub the meat with salt and pepper. Place on a rack in a roasting pan. Insert a meat thermometer with its point in the centre of the thickest part of the roast, but not against the bone.

Roast in a 175°C/350°F oven until the thermometer shows 70–72°C/158–162°F for medium rare, or 77°C/171°F for well done. Allow for 1½–2 hours' cooking time.

Herb butter: Cream the butter. Add the other ingredients. Form the butter into a cylinder and wrap it in moistened greaseproof paper. Chill. Cut it into slices.

Take out the roast and let it rest for a while. Carve it.

Serve with the herb butter, potatoes (boiled, baked, or fried raw), and for instance French beans or a salad.

Baked potatoes can be cooked in the oven at the same time as the meat. Place well-scrubbed potatoes in the oven when about 1 hour remains of the roasting time.

Roast Loin of Pork 4 servings

0.75–1 kg/1⅔–2¼ lb pork loin
1 tsp salt
- *¼ tsp white or black pepper*
  ½ tsp sage
  grated rind of 1 lemon (well scrubbed)
  1 tbs lemon juice
- *1 tsp ground ginger*
  ¼ tsp white or black pepper
- *10 stoned prunes*
  ¼ tsp white or black pepper
  ½ tsp rosemary
- *75 ml/2⅔ fl oz/⅓ cup chopped*
  parsley
  ¼ tsp white or black pepper
  1 tsp chevril

● *With Lemon and Sage:*
Rub the meat with salt and spices. Sprinkle with grated lemon rind and juice.

● *With Ginger:*
Rub the meat with salt and spices.

● *With Prunes:*
Make an incision along the bones. Stuff with prunes. Rub the meat with salt and spices.

● *With Parsley:*
Make an incision along the bones. Stuff with parsley. Rub with salt and spices

Place the meat, fatty side up, on a rack in a roasting pan. Insert a meat thermometer from the end with its point in the centre of the meat but not against any bone. Roast in a 175°C/350°F oven until the thermometer shows 82–85°C/180–185°F, 1½–2 hours.
Take out the meat and let it rest for a while.
Cut the meat away from the bones and slice it.
Serve with boiled or baked potatoes (see Roast Leg of Pork, page 130), boiled Brussels sprouts or broccoli, a salad, and apple sauce (optional).

Roast Elk with Cream Sauce 6–8 servings

1 kg/2¼ lb boneless elk (moose), eg.
from the haunch (reindeer or venison
may be used as substitutes)
2 tbs butter
1½ tsp salt
¼ tsp white or black pepper
10 crushed juniper berries

Sauce:
300 ml/½ pt/1¼ cups water or stock
100 ml/3½ fl oz/scant ½ cup cream
2 tbs rowan or redcurrant jelly
2 tbs flour + 50 ml/1¾ fl oz/scant ¼ cup
water
salt and pepper
crushed juniper berries (optional)

Place the meat on a rack in a roasting pan. Melt the butter and add salt, pepper, and crushed juniper berries. Brush the meat with this mixture. Insert a meat thermometer with its point in the centre of the meat.
Roast in a 175°C/350°F oven until the thermometer shows 77°C/171°F. Allow for 1½–2 hours' roasting time. If the meat is frozen, it may be roasted unthawed or half-thawed in a 150°C/300°F oven. The roasting time will then be about 3 hours. Insert the thermometer after 1.5 hours.
Sauce: Strain the roasting juices into a saucepan and add water or stock to make up 300 ml (½ pt/1¼ cups). Add cream and jelly. Simmer on low heat for about 5 min. Mix flour and water and beat it into the gravy. Boil for another 3–5 min. Season with salt and pepper and optional juniper berries.
Slice the meat thinly. Serve with the sauce, boiled potatoes, and Brussels sprouts.

Roast Leg of Venison   8 servings

1 bone-in joint of venison, 2–2.5
  kg/4½–5½ lb
2 tsp salt
½ tsp white or black pepper
1 tsp sage (optional)

Sauce:
300 ml/½ pt/1¼ cups water or stock
2 tbs flour + 50 ml/1¾ fl oz/scant ¼ cup
  water
100 ml/3½ fl oz/scant ½ cup cream
salt and pepper (optional)

Rub the meat with salt, pepper, and optional sage. Place on a rack in a roasting pan. Insert a meat thermometer with its point in the centre of the thickest part of the meat, but not against the bone.

Roast in a 175°C/350°F oven until the thermometer shows 70–72°C/158–162°F for medium rare or 77°C/171°F for well done. Allow for 1½–2 hours' roasting time.

If the meat is frozen, it may be roasted unthawed of half-thawed in a 150°C/300°F oven. Allow for a longer roasting time and insert the meat thermometer after 1 hour's roasting.

Deglaze the roasting pan with a little water or stock.

Sauce: Strain the roasting juices into a saucepan and add water or stock to make up 300 ml (½ pt/1¼ cups). Bring to the boil. Mix flour and water and beat it into the gravy. Add the cream. Boil for 3–5 min. Season with salt and pepper, if needed. Cut the meat away from the bone and slice it thinly.

Serve with the sauce, potatoes (boiled or fried raw), a tomato or green salad, and rowan or blackcurrant jelly.

Braised Reindeer   4 servings

1 kg/2¼ lb bone-in reindeer (caribou)
  meat, eg. from the haunch
butter
1–1½ tsp salt
1 bay leaf
3–4 white peppercorns
3–4 allspice berries
5 crushed juniper berries
1 onion
1 carrot
300 ml/½ pt/1¼ cups water

Sauce:
300 ml/½ pt/1¼ cups liquid (braising
  juices + stock)
2 tbs flour + 50 ml/1¾ fl oz/scant ¼ cup
  water
100 ml/3½ fl oz/scant ½ cup cream
salt and pepper (optional)

Heat the butter in a fireproof casserole or a heavy roaster. Brown the meat on all sides. Add salt and spices. Peel the onion and the carrot, cut them in pieces, and put them in with the meat. Moisten with a little water. Cover and cook on low heat until the meat is tender, about 1½ hours. Test with a skewer. Turn the meat once or twice and add more liquid if the meat looks dry.

Remove the meat and keep warm.

Sauce: Strain the braising juices into a saucepan. Add stock to make up 300 ml (½ pt/1¼ cups). Bring to the boil. Mix flour and water, beat it into the gravy, and add the cream. Boil for 3–5 min. Season with salt and pepper, if needed.

Cut the meat away from the bone and slice it thinly.

Serve with the sauce, potatoes (boiled or fried raw), French beans, and redcurrant or rowan jelly (made from the berries of mountain ash).

The meat may also be served with Mushroom Sauce, see page 62.

Saddle of Reindeer or Venison   6 servings   *Ren- eller rådjurssadel med enbärssås*

*1.5 kg / 3 ⅓ lb saddle of reindeer (caribou)
  or venison*
1 ½ tsp salt
½ tsp white or black pepper
2 tbs melted butter

Sauce:
300 ml / ½ pt / 1 ¼ cups stock
300 ml / ½ pt / 1 ¼ cups cream
*2 ½ tbs flour + 50 ml / 1 ¾ fl oz / scant
  ¼ cup water*
10–12 crushed juniper berries
salt

If the saddle is frozen, thaw it until the surface is soft.
Cut away the outer membrane and the big back tendon.
Rub the saddle with salt and pepper. Place on a rack in a
roasting pan. Place in a preheated oven and roast at 150°C/
300°F for frozen meat, 175°C/350°F for fresh meat. After
about half an hour, insert a meat thermometer with its point
at the centre of the meat, but not against bone. Brush the
meat with melted butter a couple of times while roasting.
When the thermometer shows 59°C/138°F the meat is red,
at 61–63°C/142–145°F it is pink, and at 70–72°C/158–
162°F it is slightly pink. Allow for 1¼–1¾ hours' roasting
time. Deglaze the roasting pan with a little stock.
Sauce: Strain the roasting juices into a saucepan and add
stock to make up 300 ml (½ pt/1¼ cups). Add the cream.
Let the gravy boil down, uncovered, on moderate heat for
8–10 min. Mix flour and water and whisk it into the gravy.
Simmer on low heat for another 3–5 min. Add juniper berries. Season with salt.
Cut the meat away from the bone and slice it. Arrange the
meat on the bones, so that the saddle looks whole.
Serve with boiled potatoes, French beans, and rowan jelly.

Marinated Pot Roast of Beef or Elk   6–8 servings   *Surstek av nöt eller älg*

*1 kg / 2 ¼ lb boneless beef or elk (moose),
  for ex. silverside or bottom round*

Marinade:
1 bottle red wine, 75 cl
*100 ml / 3 ½ fl oz / scant ½ cup red wine
  vinegar*
100 ml / 3 ½ fl oz / scant ½ cup cooking oil
2 onions, red ones if possible
10 allspice berries
10 white peppercorns
3–4 bay leaves

For the braising:
butter
1 tsp salt
*200 ml / 7 fl oz / good ¾ cup each
  marinade and water*

Sauce:
400 ml / 14 fl oz / 1 ⅔ cups braising juices
*2 ½ tbs flour + 50 ml / 1 ¾ fl oz / scant
  ¼ cup water*
100 ml / 3 ½ fl oz / scant ½ cup cream

Place the meat in a deep, closefitting basin.
Mix wine, vinegar, and oil. Peel and slice the onions. Crush
the spices lightly. Put spices and onions in the basin. Pour
the marinade over the meat, so that it is completely
covered. Put on a small plate with a weight to keep the
meat well covered with marinade. Leave in a cold place for
1–3 weeks. A longer marinating time gives a stronger
flavour. Turn the meat a few times while marinating.
Drain and dry the meat.
Heat a little butter in a fireproof casserole or a roaster and
brown the meat all around. Sprinkle with salt.
Strain and keep the marinade. Moisten the meat with a little
marinade and water. Cover and cook on low heat until the
meat is tender, about 1½ hours. Test with a skewer. Add
more liquid if needed. Remove the meat and keep warm.
Sauce: Strain the juices and add enough water to make up
400 ml (14 fl oz/1⅔ cups). Bring to the boil.
Mix flour and water and beat it into the gravy. Add the
cream. Boil for 3–5 min. Season with salt and pepper.
Cut the meat into thin slices. Serve with boiled potatoes,
lingonberry jam or cucumber salad, and a green salad.

Braised Hare 6–8 servings

1 hare, skinned and drawn, about 2.5 kg/5½ lb
1–1.5 l/1¾–2⅔ pts/4¼–6⅓ cups milk
butter
2–2½ tsp salt
½ tsp white or black pepper
400 ml/14 fl oz/1⅔ cups stock
sprigs of parsley

Sauce:
500 ml/18 fl oz/good 2 cups braising juices and stock
3 tbs flour + 50 ml/1¾ fl oz/scant ¼ cup water
150–200 ml/5–7 fl oz/⅔–¾ cup cream
soy sauce (optional)
redcurrant or rowan jelly, port or sherry

Rinse the hare well and remove any membranes and sinews. Cut off the legs and break the backbone in one or two places. Put the meat in a basin and pour in enough milk to cover. Leave in a cold place for 12 hours.

Drain and dry the meat. Heat a little butter in a fireproof casserole or a roaster. Brown the meat on all sides. Sprinkle with salt and pepper. Moisten with a little stock. Add a few sprigs of parsley.

Cover and cook on low heat until the meat is tender. If needed, add more stock. Allow for 1½–2 hours' cooking time. Test with a skewer. Remove the meat and keep warm.

Sauce: Strain the braising juices. Add stock to make up 500 ml (18 fl oz/good 2 cups). Bring to the boil. Mix flour and water and whisk it into the gravy. Add the cream. Boil for 3–5 min.

Season with optional soy sauce, jelly, or wine.

Carve the meat. Serve with the sauce, potatoes (boiled or fried raw), redcurrant or rowan jelly (made from the berries of mountain ash), cucumber salad, and Brussels sprouts.

Stuffed, Rolled Lamb 5–6 servings

1 kg/2¼ lb boned breast of lamb
1½ tsp salt
½ tsp white or black pepper

Stuffing:
1 onion
200 g/7 oz fresh or tinned chanterelles
butter
100 ml/3½ fl oz/scant ½ cup chopped parsley
200 ml/7 fl oz/good ¾ cup water, stock, or mushroom liquor

Sauce:
300 ml/½ pt/1¼ cups braising juices and stock
2 tbs flour + 50 ml/1¾ fl oz/scant ¼ cup water
50 ml/1¾ fl oz/scant ¼ cup cream
salt and pepper (optional)

Rub the meat with salt and pepper.

Stuffing: Peel and chop the onion. Cut the chanterelles into small pieces. Heat a little butter in a frying pan and fry onion and chanterelles.

Distribute onion, chanterelles, and parsley over the meat. Roll up and tie with cotton string.

Heat a little butter in a fireproof casserole or a roaster.

Brown the meat all around. Moisten with a little water, stock, or mushroom liquor. Cover and cook on low heat for 1–1½ hours.

Add more liquid if needed.

Take out the meat and keep hot.

Sauce: Strain the juices. Add stock to make up 300 ml (½ pt/1¼ cups). Bring to the boil. Mix flour and water and beat it into the gravy. Add the cream. Boil for 3–5 min. Season with salt and pepper, if needed.

Cut the meat into slices. Serve with the sauce, boiled potatoes, French beans, and a salad.

Roast Leg of Pork with Cloves and Roast Loin of Pork with Prunes.

Pork Tenderloin with Herb Sauce 4 servings *Grisfilé med örtkryddad sås*

500 g / 1 lb 2 oz pork tenderloin
butter
1–1 ½ tsp salt
½ tsp white or black pepper

Sauce:
200 ml / 7 fl oz / good ¾ cup each stock
  and cream
1 ½ tbs flour + 50 ml / 1 ¾ fl oz / scant
  ¼ cup water
50 ml / 3 rounded tbs chopped parsley
½ tsp chevril
½ tsp tarragon

Cut the meat in 2–3 cm (¾–1¼ in) slices. Flatten the slices lightly with your hand. Heat a little butter in a frying pan and fry, a few slices at a time, on moderately high heat, 2–3 min. each side. Sprinkle with salt and pepper. Arrange the meat on a serving dish and keep warm.
Sauce: Deglaze the pan with a little stock. Strain the juices into a saucepan. Add stock to make up 200 ml (7 fl oz/ good ¾ cup). Add the cream. Boil down, uncovered, on moderately high heat for 8–10 min. Mix flour and water and beat it into the gravy. Boil for 3–5 min. Add parsley, chevril, and tarragon. Season with salt and pepper.
Pour the sauce over the meat.
Serve with boiled potatoes, vegetables, or a salad.

Lamb Chops with Herb Butter 4 servings *Lammkotletter med kryddsmör*

8 single or 4 double lamb chops, butter
1–1 ½ tsp salt
¼ tsp white or black pepper

Herb butter:
50 g / 1 ¾ oz / scant ¼ cup butter
50 ml / 3 rounded tbs finely chopped
  parsley
1 tsp lemon juice

Start by making the herb butter: Cream the butter. Add parsley and lemon juice. Form the butter into a cylinder. Wrap in moistened greaseproof paper or foil. Chill until serving. Cut into slices. It can also be served soft, in a bowl. Make a couple of small cuts in the fatty edge of each chop. Heat the butter in a frying pan and fry the chops on moderately high heat, 2–3 min. each side. Sprinkle with salt and pepper.
Serve with the herb butter, potatoes (boiled of fried raw), boiled vegetables, or a salad.

Beef Olives (Beef Roulades) 4 servings *Nötrulader*

8 thin slices of boneless beef, eg. topside
  or silverside, top or bottom round,
  about 500 g / 1 lb 2 oz
1 small tin Swedish anchovy fillets (or
  anchovies in oil), about 50 g / 1 ¾ oz
1 small onion
butter
½–1 tsp salt
¼ tsp white or black pepper

Sauce:
300 ml / ½ pt / 1 ¼ cups stock
2 tbs flour + 50 ml / 1 ¾ fl oz / scant ¼ cup
  water
100 ml / 3 ½ fl oz / scant ½ cup cream
soy sauce
salt and pepper (optional)

Beef Olives (Beef Roulades).

Drain the anchovy fillets and cut them into pieces. Peel and finely chop the onion. Spread out the meat slices on a carving board. Distribute anchovies and onion over them. Roll up the slices and fasten with toothpicks.
Heat a little butter in a frying pan. Brown the beef olives on all sides. Sprinkle with salt and pepper. Moisten with a little stock. Cover and cook on low heat until the meat is tender, ¾–1 hour. Arrange the beef olives on a serving dish and keep warm. Remove the toothpicks.
Sauce: Strain the pan juices and add stock to make up 300 ml (½ pt / 1 ¼ cups). Mix flour and water and whisk it into the gravy. Add the cream. Boil for 3–5 min. Season with soy sauce and with salt and pepper if needed.
Pour the sauce over the beef olives. Serve with boiled potatoes, boiled vegetables, or a salad.

Pork Roulades 4 servings

8 thin slices of rind- and bone-less fresh
   ham or pork shoulder, about 600 g/1
   ⅓ lb
1–1½ tsp salt
¼ tsp white or black pepper
butter

Filling:
- with apples and prunes:
   1 tart apple, peeled, cored, and cut
   into thin wedges
   8 stoned prunes, cut into strips
   ¼ tsp ground ginger

- with mushrooms and parsley:
   100 g/3½ oz fresh mushrooms,
   coarsely chopped
   50 ml/3 rounded tbs chopped parsley
   1 tbs finely grated lemon rind or
   lemon juice
   ½ tsp chervil

Sauce:
300 ml/½ pt/1¼ cups stock
2 tbs flour + 50 ml/1¾ fl oz/scant ¼ cup
water
100 ml/3½ fl oz/scant ½ cup cream
soy sauce
salt and pepper (optional)

Prepare one of the fillings.
Spread out the meat slices on a carving board.
Sprinkle with salt and pepper. Distribute the filling on them.
Roll up and fasten with toothpicks.
Heat a little butter in a frying pan and brown the roulades on all sides. Moisten with a little stock. Cover and cook on low heat until the meat is tender, about 15 min. Arrange the roulades on a serving dish and keep warm. Remove the toothpicks.
Sauce: Strain the pan juices and add stock to make up 300 ml (½ pt/1¼ cups). Mix flour and water and beat it into the gravy. Add the cream. Boil for 3–5 min. Season with soy sauce and with salt and pepper if needed.
Pour the sauce over the roulades. Serve with boiled potatoes, boiled vegetables, or a salad.

Wallenbergers 4 servings

400 g/14 oz minced veal or lean pork
3 egg yolks
200 ml/7 fl oz/good ¾ cup whipping
   cream
1 tsp salt
¼ tsp white or black pepper
butter

These luxurious veal patties are named after the Wallenberg family (famous Swedish financiers and industrialists). The original recipe comes from Amalia Wallenberg, who was the daughter of Ch. E. Hagdahl, a great writer on culinary art.

Blend the minced meat with egg yolks, cream, salt, and pepper to a soft mixture.
Brown a little butter in a frying pan. With a spoon place dollops of the mixture directly in the frying pan. Fry on rather low heat, about 2 min. each side. Serve at once with mashed potatoes, green peas, and a salad.

Wallenbergers with Green Pees.

Beefsteak (Steamboat Steak)   4 servings

Biffstek (Ångbåtsbiff)

*4 beefsteaks, from the uppercut of the
   loin (top round)*
4 onions, red ones if available
butter
1 tsp salt
¼ tsp white or black pepper
stock or water (optional)

Peel and slice the onions. Brown them in butter in a frying pan. Reduce the heat and fry until soft, stirring all the time. Season with salt and pepper. Remove the onions and keep warm. Deglaze the pan with a little stock and pour it over the onions.

Brown a little butter in the frying pan. Fry the steaks on rather high heat, 1½–3 min. each side. Sprinkle with salt and pepper after frying. Arrange the steaks on a hot serving dish.

Pour the hot pan juices over the steaks.

Serve at once with fried or boiled potatoes and a salad.

Calf's Tongue in Madeira Sauce 4 servings *Kalvtunga i madeirasauce*

1 lightly salted calf's tongue, about 500
  g/1 lb 2 oz
6–8 white peppercorns
1 bay leaf
1 carrot
1 onion or 1 piece of leek

Sauce:
1½ tbs butter
1½ tbs flour
300 ml/½ pt/1¼ cups stock
1 tbs tomato purée
50 ml/1¾ fl oz/scant ¼ cup Madeira
soy sauce (optional)
salt and pepper (optional)

Place the tongue in a saucepan. Add enough water to cover. Bring to the boil and skim well. Add peppercorns and bay leaf. Peel the carrot and cut it in pieces. Rinse the leek. Put the vegetables in the saucepan. Cover and simmer on low heat until the tongue is very tender, 1–1½ hours. Test with a skewer.

Remove the tongue and skin it. Return it to the saucepan and keep it hot in its cooking liquid.

Sauce: Melt the butter in a saucepan. Blend in the flour. Thin with the stock while stirring. Add the tomato purée and boil for 3–5 min. Season with Madeira, soy sauce, and optional salt and pepper.

Take out the tongue and cut it in thin slices.

Serve with the sauce, boiled, riced potatoes, and vegetables, eg. asparagus and small green peas.

Fried Liver *Stekt lever med olika tillbehör*

500 g/1 lb 2 oz calf's liver
2 tbs flour
1 tsp salt
¼ tsp white or black pepper
butter

Serving suggestions:
- 100 ml/3½ fl oz/scant ½ cup pickled
  beetroots
  50 ml/3 rounded tbs capers
- about 100 g/3½ oz bacon, cut into
  strips and fried crisp
- lingonberry jam
  soured cream
- fried onions (sliced)
- finely shredded leek
  grated lemon rind

Trim the liver and remove any membranes and sinews. Dry. Cut in 2 cm (¾ in) slices. Mix flour, salt, and pepper and turn the liver slices in this mixture.

Heat a little butter in a frying pan and fry the slices until nicely browned, about 3 min. each side. Arrange on a warmed serving dish.

Distribute the chosen garnish on top of the liver.

Serve with boiled potatoes and a green salad.

Roasted Lamb's Liver 4 servings

500 g/1 lb 2 oz lamb's liver
1 tsp salt
¼ tsp white or black pepper
½ tsp thyme

Sauce:
1 tbs butter
1½ tbs flour
200 ml/7 fl oz/good ¾ cup stock
150 ml/¼ pt/⅔ cup cream
salt and pepper
soy sauce (optional)

Remove any membranes and sinews from the liver. Dry. Rub with salt, pepper, and thyme. Place the liver on a rack in a roasting tin. Roast in a 175°C/350°F oven until just done, about 35 min.

Sauce: Melt the butter in a saucepan. Blend in the flour. Thin with stock and cream while stirring. Boil for 3–5 min. Season with salt, pepper, and optional soy sauce.

Cut the liver into thin slices.

Serve with the sauce, boiled potatoes, French beans, and pickled cucumbers.

Sautéed Kidneys 4 servings

400 g/14 oz calves' or lambs' kidneys
water
2 tsp salt per litre/1¾ pts/4¼ cups water
200 g/7 oz fresh, frozen, or tinned
  mushrooms
2 tbs butter
1 tsp salt
¼ tsp white or black pepper
2 tbs flour
150 ml/¼ pt/⅔ cup each stock and
  cream
2 tbs sherry (optional)

Blanch the kidneys: put them in a saucepan, pour in enough water to cover. Add salt. Bring to the boil. Pour off the water. Finely dice the kidneys. Rinse and slice fresh mushrooms or drain tinned ones.

Fry kidneys and mushrooms, a little at a time, in a frying pan. Return all to the pan. Season with salt and pepper. Blend in the flour. Thin with stock and cream while stirring. Simmer on low heat for about 5 min.

Season with optional sherry.

Serve in warmed shortcrust or puff pastry shells, on toast, or on boiled celeriac slices (celery-root), with a green salad.

Reindeer Roulades

200 ml/7 fl oz/good ¾ cup whipping
  cream
1–2 tbs grated horseradish
50 ml/3 rounded tbs finely chopped
  parsley
100 g/3½ oz thinly sliced smoked rein-
  deer meat

Whip the cream. Season with horseradish and parsley. Spoon a little of the cream on to each slice of meat. Roll up the meat around the cream filling.

Serve chilled as a first course, accompanied by a green salad.

Rolled Reindeer Sandwich 4 sandwiches

1 round of soft flatbread
1½–2 tbs butter
½ tbs grated horseradish
100 g/3½ oz thinly sliced smoked rein-
  deer meat

Cream the butter and season it with horseradish. Divide the flatbread into 4 pieces. Spread with the horseradish-butter. Put the meat on top. Roll up the bread to form a cone. Flatten the cone somewhat.

POULTRY AND GAME BIRDS

Roast Turkey   8 servings

Stekt kalkon

1 mini-turkey, 2.5–3.5 kg/5½–7¾ lb
2 tsp salt
½ tsp white or black pepper
2–3 tsp melted butter

Sauce:
400 ml/14 oz/1 ⅔ cups roasting juices
*   and stock*
3 tbs flour + 50 ml/1¾ fl oz/scant ¼ cup
*   water*
200 ml/7 fl oz/good ¾ cup cream
salt and pepper

Thaw a frozen turkey enough that the package of giblets can be pulled out. Season outside and inside with salt and pepper.
Place the turkey on its side on a rack in a roasting tin. Brush with melted butter.
Roast in a 175°C/350°F oven for about 30 min. Turn the bird and roast for another 30 min. Now turn the turkey breast-up and continue roasting until the bird is done. Brush with melted butter from time to time. Allow for a total roasting time of 1½–2 hours. Test for doneness by pricking the tigh deeply with a fork. When the juices run clear and yellow the bird is done. Remove the turkey and deglaze the roasting tin with a little water.
Sauce: Strain the roasting juices and add enough stock to make up 400 ml (14 fl oz/1⅔ cups). Bring to the boil. Mix flour and water and beat it into the gravy. Add the cream. Boil for 3–5 min. Season with salt and pepper.
Carve the turkey. Serve with the sauce, boiled potatoes, or roast potatoes in wedges (see page 54), Brussels sprouts, and a green salad.

Pot Roast of Chicken   4 servings

Grytstekt kyckling

1 fresh chicken, about 1 kg/2¼ lb
1 tsp salt
½ tsp white or black pepper
parsley
butter
about 200 ml/7 fl oz/good ¾ cup stock

Sauce:
300 ml/½ pt/1¼ cups braising juices and
*   stock*
200 ml/7 fl oz/good ¾ cup cream
2 tbs flour + 50 ml/1¾ fl oz/scant ¼ cup
*   water*

Rub the chicken with salt and pepper. Fill with coarsely chopped parsley. Heat a little butter in a fireproof casserole or roaster and brown the chicken all around. Moisten with a little stock. Cover and cook on low heat until done, about 30 min. Baste from time to time. Remove the chicken.
Sauce: Strain the juices and add enough stock to make up 300 ml (½ pt/1¼ cups). Add the cream. Bring to the boil. Mix flour and water and beat it into the gravy. Boil for 3–5 min.
Season with salt and pepper.
Carve the chicken. Serve with the sauce, boiled potatoes, cucumber salad, and a mixed salad.

Roast Chicken with Cream Sauce.

Roast Chicken   4 servings

1 chicken (fresh or frozen), about 1 kg/2¼ lb
1 tsp salt
¼–½ tsp white or black pepper
1 tsp ground dried herbs, eg. chevril, tarragon, or rosemary
2 tbs melted butter

Thaw the frozen chicken enough that the package of giblets can be pulled out. Rub with salt and pepper all over the bird. Place the chicken on a rack in a roasting pan. Brush with melted butter.

Roast in a 175°C/350°F oven until the chicken is tender, 50–60 min. Serve with roast potatoes in halves or wedges (see page 54) and a salad.

Roast Duck   4–6 servings

1 duck, 1.5–2 kg/3⅓–4½ lb
½ lemon
2 tsp salt
¼–½ tsp white or black pepper
2–3 apples

Sauce:
300 ml/½ pt/1¼ cups roasting juices and stock
2 tsp arrowroot or potato flour + 2 tbs water
salt and pepper

Thaw the duck if it is frozen. Rub it with lemon inside and outside. Season with salt and pepper. Rinse the apples and cut them into wedges. Stuff the duck with the apples. Close the vent with skewers or sew up with cotton string.
Place the duck back upwards on a rack in a roasting pan. Roast in a 175°C/350°F oven. After about 30 min. turn the duck breast-up and continue roasting for another hour.
Test for doneness by pricking the tigh with a fork. When the juices run clear and yellow, the duck is done. Remove the bird and keep warm. Deglaze the roasting pan with a little water.
Sauce: Strain the juices and skim away the fat. Add enough stock to make up 300 ml (½ pt/1¼ cups). Bring to the boil. Mix arrowroot or potato flour with the water and beat it into the gravy. Bring back to the boil. Season with salt and pepper.
Carve the duck. Serve with the sauce, redcurrant jelly, or cucumber salad, potatoes (boiled or fried raw), and boiled vegetables.

Variation: *Duck with Orange Sauce*   *Anka med apelsinsås*
Roast the duck as described above. Thinly peel a well-scrubbed orange. Cut the rind into thin strips. Boil in the stock for about 5 min. Mix arrowroot or potatoflour with the orange juice and whisk it into the sauce. Bring back to the boil.
Season with salt and pepper.

Salted Goose   8–10 servings

1 goose, 4–5 kg/9–11 lb

Brine:
5 l/9 pts/good 5 quarts water
500 g/1 lb 2 oz/1⅔ cups salt
85 g/3 oz/scant ½ cup sugar
1 tbs saltpetre (optional)

For the boiling:
water
1 onion
10 white peppercorns
1 bay leaf

Thaw a frozen goose enough that the package of giblets can be pulled out.

Mix water, salt, sugar, and optional saltpetre together in a saucepan. Bring to the boil and set aside to cool.

Place the goose in a bowl. Pour in the brine. There should be enough brine to cover the bird. Leave in a cold place for about 48 hours. Take out the goose and dry it.

Place the goose breast-up in a pot. Pour on enough water, so that the bird is just covered. Add the giblets. Bring to the boil and skim carefully.

Peel the onion. Add onion, peppercorns, and bay leaf to the pot. Cover and simmer on low heat for 1½–2 hours. Test with a fork or a skewer.

The goose may be served hot or cold. If it is to be served cold, cool it as quickly as possible in its cooking liquid.

Carve the goose. Serve hot with boiled potatoes, red cabbage, and a salad, or cold with soured cream, seasoned with horseradish, boiled potatoes, and a salad.

Variation: *Salted Turkey*   *Språngd kalkon*

Proceed as described in the master recipe. Estimated cooking time is about 1 hour for a turkey weighing 2.5–3.5 kg/5½–7¾ lb.

Pot Roast of Game Birds   4 servings

1 wild duck, or 1 pheasant, or 2 grouse
  (plucked, drawn, and singed)
butter
1½–2 tsp salt
½ tsp white or black pepper
4–5 crushed juniper berries (optional)
about 200 ml/7 fl oz/good ¾ cup stock

Sauce:
300 ml/½ pt/1¼ cups braising juices and
  stock
2 tbs flour + 50 ml/1¾ fl oz/scant
  ¼ cup water
100 ml/3½ fl oz/scant ½ cup cream
salt and pepper
1–2 tbs blackcurrant jelly

Thaw the birds if they are frozen. Truss with cotton string. Heat a little butter in a fireproof casserole or roaster and brown the birds on all sides. Season with salt and pepper. Moisten with a little stock. Cover and cook on low heat until the birds are tender, test with a fork or a skewer. Allow for a cooking time of about 50 min. for duck, 40–60 min. for pheasant, and 45 min. for grouse. Remove the birds and keep warm.

Sauce: Strain the juices and add enough stock to make up 300 ml (½ pt/1¼ cups). Bring to the boil. Mix flour and water and whisk it into the gravy. Add the cream. Boil for 3–5 min.

Season with salt, pepper, and blackcurrant jelly.

Carve the birds. Serve with the sauce, boiled potatoes, blackcurrant jelly, cucumber salad, and boiled vegetables.

Seasonal holidays and feasts

"At no time of the year did one eat so abundantly and so traditionally as at Christmas. If one had to lead a simple and spartan life for the rest of the year, one would gorge oneself at Christmas, when there was a plentiful supply of fresh food, which kept well, thanks to the cold weather. The customs were rather similar within the county, but for economic reasons the number of dishes on the Christmas table naturally varied." This was written by Rut Wallensteen-Jaeger in her book "Food for Workdays and Feasts", which describes the food traditions in Östergötland at the beginning of the century.

The Christmas food has been and still is very important to most people. Then, more than ever, one wants to have the dishes one knows from one's childhood. In many young families food traditions from both parental homes are mixed and developed into new traditions.

It is no longer very profitable to make sausages, brawn, and pâté at home, but there is a very valuable feeling of togetherness when the whole family, maybe several generations, works together preparing the Christmas food. The flavour of homemade food can not be calculated in money either.

The other festivals do not show such a rich variety of traditional dishes. Easter has only a few. The salmon pudding on God Friday is not so common nowadays as the boiled eggs on Holy Saturday. Midsummer means new potatoes, herrings and chives, and often a cake, decorated with the first Swedish strawberries. The crayfish has many enthusiasts, and so has the November goose. The succession of seasonal dishes may contribute to an enhanced awareness of time and may lead us to collect good food memories year by year.

CHRISTMAS

Christmas preparations start early in Sweden. There is a lot to do: gifts and decorations are bought or made, plenty of food is prepared. The preparations take on a festive air. Even the most anti-traditional people observe a few Christmas traditions.

Herring Salad
Sillsallad

2 de-salted salt herring fillets
2 cold boiled potatoes
1 apple
1 pickled cucumber
6 medium-sized pickled beetroots or
   about 400 ml/14 fl oz/1⅔ cups diced
   pickled beetroots
100 ml/3½ fl oz/scant ½ cup whipping
   cream or 150 ml/¼ pt/⅔ cup soured
   cream

Garnish:
2 hard-boiled eggs

Finely dice herring, potatoes, the peeled and cored apple, the cucumber, and the beetroots. Mix all together. Chill for a few hours before serving.

Mix the salad with whipped cream or soured cream. Garnish with hard-boiled eggs, cut in wedges.

Variation: *Beetroot Salad*   *Rödbetssallad*
Omit herring and potatoes in the above recipe. The quantity of apple and cucumber may be increased somewhat. Season the cream or soured cream with ½–1 tbs grated horseradish.

Pork Sausages

1 l/1¾ pts/4¼ cups milk
90 g/3¼ oz/⅔ cup flour
1 onion
2.5 kg/5½ lb boneless pork
2 tsp white pepper
¼ tsp ground ginger (optional)
60 g/good 2 oz/⅓ cup potato flour

Brine:
3 l/5½ pts/good 3 quarts water
200 g/7 oz fine or coarse salt without iodine
2 tbs sugar
about 5 m/16 feet intestines (soaked overnight in cold water)

Bring 800 ml (scant 1½ pts/3⅓ cups) of the milk to the boil. Mix the rest of the milk with the flour. Blend this thickening into the hot milk. Simmer for 3–5 min., stirring continously. Set aside until completely cold.

Peel the onion and cut it into pieces. Cut the meat into pieces. Put meat and onion together trough the mincer three times. Mix the minced meat with the cold white sauce, the spices and the potato flour.

Blend vigorously, preferably using an electric mixing machine. Poach a small spoonful of the sausage meat in lightly salted water to check the seasoning. Add more spices if needed.

N.B. There is no salt included in the sausage meat.

Stuff the intestines rather loosely. Tie into suitable lengths.

For the brine, bring water, salt, and sugar to the boil. Leave to cool.

Place the sausages in a large bowl or a bucket (preferably stainless steel). Pour over the cold brine.

Put a plate on top of the sausages to keep them down. Leave in a cold place for about 24 hours.

The sausages may then be stored in the brine for about a week if kept in a cold place. In this case the brine should be changed on the second day and the sausages must be soaked in water for a couple of hours before boiling.

To boil the sausages, put them either in the stock from the Christmas ham or in water with some allspice berries and bay leaves. Cover and simmer on low heat for about 30 min. After boiling you may freeze the sausages.

Sausage from Värmland

1.5 kg/3⅓ lb boneless beef
1.5 kg/3⅓ lb boneless pork
3 kg/6⅔ lb raw potatoes
2 medium-sized onions, preferably red ones
2 tbs salt
½ tsp white pepper
about 5 m/16 feet intestines (soaked overnight in cold water)

Cut the meat into pieces. Peel potatoes and onions and cut them into pieces. Put meat, potatoes, and onions together through the mincer twice.

Add salt and pepper and blend vigorously. Fry a small spoonful of the mixture to check the seasoning.

Stuff the intestines rather loosely. Tie into suitable lengths.

Boil the sausages for about 30 min. in the stock used for the Christmas ham or in lightly salted water (2 tsp salt per litre/1¾ pts/4¼ cups water) with a few allspice berries and a bay leaf.

The sausages may be frozen boiled or raw, but they may also be stored raw in light brine (see the recipe for Pork Sausages).

The Swedish Christmas table is served at lunch-time on Christmas Eve. The centrepiece is a ham surrounded by various cold and hot dishes, such as pickled herring, meat balls, red cabbage, patés and salads. The lutfisk and rice porridge shown here are usually served as supper.

Pork Sausages with Barley

Orökta isterband (grynkorv)

about 350 g/12 oz/2 cups pearl barley
1.5 l/2⅔ pts/6⅓ cups water
1 onion
2 kg/4½ lb minced pork
2 tbs salt
1 tbs sugar
1 tsp ground allspice
about 5 m/16 feet intestines, soaked
    overnight in cold water

Place the pearl barley in a saucepan with the water. Cover and simmer on low heat, until all the water has been absorbed and the barley seems soft, about 30 min. Leave until completely cold.

Peel the onion and chop it finely or grate it. Mix the minced meat with the cold barley, onion, salt, sugar, and allspice.

Fry a small spoonful of the mixture to check the seasoning. Add more spices if needed.

Stuff the intestines rather loosely. Tie into suitable lengths and tie each length into a ring. Hang the rings on a stick in a cold and well-ventilated place overnight. The surface of the sausages will dry up and the flavour will mature and become slightly tart.

Boil the sausages in the stock used for the Christmas ham, or in lightly salted water (2 tsp salt per litre/1¾ pts/4¼ cups water) for about 20 min.

They may also be cut into pieces and fried.

The sausages may be frozen, raw or boiled.

Pressed Rolled Pork

Rullsylta

2 kg/4½ lb fresh lean belly pork
1 tsp salt
1 tsp crushed white peppercorns
1 tsp crushed allspice berries
½ tsp crushed cloves

Brine:
100 g/3½ oz fine or coarse salt without
    iodine
1 tbs sugar
2 l/3½ pts/8½ cups water
1 tsp saltpetre (optional)

For the boiling:
water
1 carrot
1 onion
10 white or black peppercorns

Lay the pork flat and cut it in half, horisontally, but let the two halves stick together.

Mix salt and spices and scatter them evenly over the pork. Roll up the pork firmly, skinside out. Tie with cotton string. Mix the ingredients for the brine in a basin. Stir until salt and sugar are dissolved.

Leave the rolled pork in the brine for about 48 hours in a cold place (a really cool larder in winter, otherwise in the refrigerator). Put a weight on top of the roll to keep it down. Remove the roll and put it in a pot. Add enough water to cover. Bring to the boil. Skim. Peel the carrot and the onion and cut them in pieces. Add them and the peppercorns to the pot. Simmer on low heat until tender, about 2½ hours. Remove the roll and weigh it down hard between two carving boards until cold, for instance overnight.

Cut into thin slices and serve with pickled beetroots or Beetroot Salad (see page 146).

Variation: *Rolled Lamb*   *Lammrulle*

Substitute 1 boned breast of lamb for the belly pork. Season with 2 tsp salt, 1 tsp crushed allspice berries, and 1–2 tsp marjoram. For the rest follow the above recipe, but calculate the cooking time to 1½–2 hours.

Christmas Brawn (Head Cheese)

1 pork knuckle
1 veal knuckle
water
1 tbs salt per litre/1¾ pts/4¼ cups water
1 onion
5 white peppercorns
5 allspice berries
1 bay leaf

For the spice mixture:
65 g/2¼ oz/¼ cup salt
½ tbs crushed white peppercorns
1 tbs crushed allspice berries

Rinse the knuckles. Put them in a pot. Measure the water and pour in enough to cover the meat. Add salt. Bring to the boil. Skim. Peel the onion and cut it into pieces. Add onion and spices to the pot. Cover and simmer on low heat until the meat is tender and easily comes away from the bones, 1½–2 hours.

Remove the meat and set aside to cool. Save the cooking liquid. Dip a napkin, a tea towel, or a piece of cheesecloth in hot water and wring it out. Spread it in a 1.5 l (2⅔ pts/6⅓ cups) bowl.

Pick the meat off the bones and remove rind and sinews. Cut the meat into small pieces. Arrange it on the napkin in the bowl with a sprinkling of spices between the layers of meat. Include some fatty pieces, otherwise the brawn will not stick together. Pull the cloth tightly around the meat and tie it with a string. Bring the cooking liquid back to the boil. Lower the brawn in its cloth into the liquid. Simmer on low heat for about 15 min.

Remove the brawn and put it on a plate. Put a carving board with a weight on top, to press down. Leave to cool overnight. Untie the cloth and loosen it carefully from the brawn. Cut the brawn into slices and serve with pickled beetroots.

Liver Pâté

500 g/1 lb 2 oz pig's liver
500 g/1 lb 2 oz pork fat
1 apple
1 onion
1 small tin Swedish anchovy fillets, about
*   50 g/1¾ oz*
3 eggs
250 ml/9 fl oz/good cup milk
90 g/3¼ oz/⅔ cup flour
2 tsp salt
½ tsp white pepper
¼ tsp ground ginger

Rinse the liver and remove any membranes. Cut liver and pork fat into pieces. Peel and core the apple, peel the onion.

Cut them into pieces. Drain the anchovies.

Put liver, pork fat, apple, onion, and anchovies through the mincer 3–4 times. Beat the eggs, a little of the milk, and the flour together to form a smooth batter. Add the rest of the milk. Blend the batter, salt, and spices into the liver mixture. Fry a small spoonful to check seasoning and add more spices if needed.

Turn the mixture into one or two well-buttered moulds. The total capacity should be about 1 l (1¾ pts/4¼ cups). Cover with aluminium foil. Bake in a 200°C/400°F oven until set, about 1½ hours.

Leave to cool in the mould. When cold, turn out.

Serve for instance with pickled cucumber.

The liver pâté may be frozen, raw or cooked.

Pork Aspic with Herbs

1 fresh pork knuckle, about 1.5 kg/3⅓ lb
water
2 tsp salt per litre/1¾ pts/4¼ cups water
1 carrot
1 onion
8 white peppercorns
4 allspice berries
1 tsp thyme
1 tsp marjoram

For the jelly:
700 ml/1¼ pts/3 cups stock
1 tbs plain unflavoured powdered
*   gelatine*

Place the meat in a saucepan. Measure the water and pour in enough barely to cover the meat. Add salt. Bring to the boil.

Skim well. Peel carrot and onion and cut them into pieces. Add vegetables and spices to the meat. Cover and simmer on low heat until the meat is tender and comes easily away from the bones, 1½–2 hours. Remove the meat and set aside to cool. Remove rind and bones from the meat. Cut the meat into small pieces.

Strain the stock and measure out 700 ml (1¼ pts/3 cups) in a saucepan. Soften the gelatine in 3 tbs of the stock. When softened mix with the rest of the stock and heat until the gelatine is dissolved. Pour a little of the liquid aspic in a mould (1.2 l/2 pts/5 cups capacity) and chill until set.

Arrange the meat in the mould and pour in the rest of the aspic.

Chill until completely set, 8–10 hours. Dip the mould quickly in hot water and turn out the aspic.

Serve with boiled potatoes and pickled beetroots or beetroot salad (see page 146).

Boiled Pig's Trotters (Pig's Feet) 4 servings

4 fresh or lightly salted pig's trotters
water
2 tsp salt per litre/1¾ pts/4¼ cups water
*   for fresh pig's trotters*
1 onion
5 white peppercorns
10 allspice berries
1 bay leaf

Scrape the trotters carefully. Remove any bristles and rinse well. Place in a saucepan. Measure the water and pour in enough to cover the meat. Add salt. Bring to the boil. Skim. Peel the onion and cut it into pieces. Add onion and spices to the meat. Cover and simmer on low heat until the trotters are very tender. Allow for 2½ hours' cooking.

Remove the pig's trotters and set aside to cool. Cut each trotter in two lengthwise with a sharp knife.

Arrange the pig's trotters on a serving platter. Strain the cooking liquid and pour a little over the trotters. Chill. The stock will set as it grows cold.

Serve chilled with pickled beetroots.

Lightly Salted Ham—Christmas Ham

fresh ham, with or without bones

To cure:
4 tbs salt
2 tbs sugar
½ tbs saltpetre (optional: gives a red
colour to the meat and acts as a
preservative)

For the brine:
5 l/9 pts/good 5 quarts water
900 g/2 lb fine or coarse salt without
iodine
2 tbs sugar
½ tbs saltpetre (optional)

Tie up the boneless ham with cotton string, so that it gets a nice and even shape.

Mix salt, sugar, and optional saltpetre. Rub the ham with the mixture. Leave in a cold place for 24 hours.

Mix all the ingredients for the brine in a pot. Bring to the boil. Skim. Set aside until completely cold. Place the ham in a basin. Pour the brine over the ham—it should be well covered. Turn the ham from time to time and keep it in a cold place. A big ham (7–8 kg/15–17 lb) should be left in the brine for about 3 weeks, a smaller ham (3–4 kg/6½–9 lb) for about 2 weeks.

Home-cured ham should be de-salted for a couple of hours if it is to be boiled, and for about 15 hours if it is to be baked.

Cooking a Christmas Ham

De-salt a home-cured ham as described above. A commercially cured ham should be de-salted according to the instructions on the package.

Baked Ham
Ugnsbakad skinka

Wrap the ham in aluminium foil. Place on a rack in a roasting pan. Insert a meat thermometer with its point in the centre of the thickest part, but not against the bone.

Bake in a 175°C/350°F oven, until the thermometer shows 75°C/167°F. Allow for a cooking time of 60–75 min. per kg (2¼ lb). Remove the thermometer and the foil. Cut open any net or string around the ham. Take off the rind. Allow to cool. Save the roasting juices to make dip stock.

Boiled Ham
Kokt skinka

Insert a meat thermometer with its point in the centre of the thickest part of the ham, but not against the bone. Place the ham in a pot. Pour on enough water to cover the ham. Bring to the boil and skim. Add 10 white or black peppercorns, 10 allspice berries, 1 bay leaf, and a peeled onion. Cover and simmer on very low heat, until the thermometer shows 75°C/167°F. Allow for a cooking time of 50–60 min. per kg (2¼ lb).

Take out the ham. Remove the thermometer. Cut open any net or string around the ham. Take off the rind. Allow to cool. Save the stock to be used as dip stock.

Grilled Ham
Griljerad skinka

Beat 1 egg with 50 ml (3 rounded tbs) prepared mustard. Brush the ham with this mixture.
Sprinkle with breadcrumbs.
Place the ham in a roasting tin. Brown in a 200°C/400°F oven for about 15 min.

Dip Stock
Doppspad

Thin the concentrated juices from the baked ham with stock, or boil down the cooking liquid from the boiled ham, until suitably concentrated. Strain and season with more spices if needed.

Spiced Ham

Kryddskinka

1 lightly salted, boneless ham,
  3–4 kg/6½–9 lb
3 bay leaves
2 tsp whole cloves
1 tsp allspice berries
1 tsp marjoram
1 tsp rosemary

Cut open and remove the net around the ham. Cut off the rind. Place the ham on a large sheet of aluminium foil. Pound all the spices together in a mortar. Sprinkle the spices on the ham. Wrap the foil around the ham to make a tight package. Insert a meat thermometer with its point in the centre of the thickest part of the ham. Bake in a 175°C/ 350°F oven, until the thermometer shows 75°C/167°F. Allow 60–70 min. per kg (2¼ lb) of ham.
Remove the thermometer. Leave the ham to cool in the foil if it is to be served cold. Remove foil and cut the ham in thin slices when ready to serve.

Lutfisk (Ling or cod pickled in lye)   4 servings

Lutfisk med sås

1.5–2 kg/3½–4½ lb lutfisk, ready to
  cook

Soak the fish in plenty of cold water for 2–3 hours before boiling.

Cooking in the oven:

Place the fish skinside down in a deep, ovenproof dish. Sprinkle with 3–4 tsp salt. Cover with aluminium foil. Cook in a 225°C/435°F oven for 40–55 min., depending on the thickness of the fish. Pour off any liquid that has formed.

Cooking on the stove:

Place the fish skinside down in an enamelled or stainless steel saucepan. Sprinkle with 3–4 tsp salt. Add 50–100 ml (1¾–3½ fl oz/¼–½ cup) water. Cover and poach on low heat for about 20 min. Pour off any liquid that has formed.

Supper on Christmas Eve consists of Lutfisk *and Rice Porridge or Rice à la Malta. The* Lutfisk *is boiled and served with boiled potatoes, green peas, and a béchamel sauce flavoured with mustard, pepper, or allspice.*

Sauce:
2 tbs butter
3 tbs flour
500 ml / 18 fl oz / good 2 cups milk
100 ml / 3½ fl oz / scant ½ cup cream
1–1½ tsp salt
½ tsp white or black pepper
2–3 tbs Scanian mustard (a strong
*   coarsely-ground, prepared mustard,*
*   similar to the German old-fashioned*
*   mustard) (optional)*

Sauce: Melt the butter in a saucepan. Blend in the flour. Thin with milk and cream. Simmer on low heat for 3–5 min., stirring from time to time. Season with salt, pepper, and optional mustard.

Serve the *lutfisk* with the sauce, boiled potatoes, ground allspice, white or black pepper, and green peas.

Lutfisk Soufflé 4 servings

45 g/1½ oz/scant ¼ cup rice
2 tbs butter
3 tbs flour
200 ml/7 fl oz/good ¾ cup milk
1–1½ tsp salt
¼ tsp white or black pepper
4 egg yolks
about 400 ml/14 fl oz/1⅔ cups boiled
  lutfisk
4 egg whites

Boil the rice in lightly salted water according to the instructions on the packet. Pour off any remaining water and set aside to cool.

Melt the butter in a saucepan. Blend in the flour and thin with the milk. Boil for 3–5 min. Season with salt and pepper. Blend in the egg yolks, one at a time, and then the rice. Divide the fish into small pieces and add them. Beat the egg whites to stiff peaks and fold them into the cold soufflé base. Turn into a well-buttered soufflé mould.

Bake in a 175°C/350°F oven for 40–50 min.

Serve with broccoli or French beans and creamed butter.

Roasted Spareribs 4 servings

1 kg/2¼ lb thickly-cut spareribs
1½ tsp salt
¼ tsp white or black pepper
½–1 tsp ground ginger
2 tbs melted butter

Rub the spareribs with salt and spices. Place them fleshy side up on a rack in a roasting pan. Brush with melted butter. Roast in a 175°C/350°F oven for about 1½ hours. Turn the spareribs, brush with butter once while cooking.

Serve with boiled prunes, apple sauce, or boiled apple halves, and red cabbage (see page 157).

Variation: *Lightly Salted Spareribs*   *Rimmade revbensspjäll*

Brine: 2 l (3½ pts/8½ cups) water, 375 (13 oz) fine or coarse salt without iodine, 1 tbs sugar.

To roast: ¼ tsp white or black pepper, ½ tsp ground ginger, 2 tbs melted butter.

Mix water, salt, and sugar for the brine. Stir until salt and sugar are dissolved. Put in the spareribs. Put on a weight to keep the meat down. Leave in a cold place for about 15 hours. Remove the meat, drain, and dry. Season, brush with melted butter, and roast as described in the master recipe, but omit the salt.

Creamed Kale 4–6 servings

2 medium-sized heads of kale or 2 pack-
  ets frozen kale, 375 g/13 oz each
200 ml/7 fl oz/good ¾ cup stock from
  the ham
butter
150–200 ml/5–7 fl oz/⅔–¾ cup cream
¼ tsp white pepper
½ tsp salt (optional)
¼ tsp sugar (optional)

Rinse the fresh kale. Strip the leaves off the tough stalks.

Boil the kale in the stock for about 40 min. Remove the kale, drain, and chop. Or, boil the frozen kale in the stock for about 20 min. Drain carefully.

Heat a little butter in a saucepan and fry the kale. Thin with the cream.

Simmer kale and cream on low heat for about 15 min. Stir from time to time. Season with white pepper and optional salt and sugar. Serve as an accompaniment to ham or sausages.

Red Cabbage   4 servings

1 head of red cabbage (0.75–1 kg/1 ½–2 ¼ lb)
3–4 tart apples
1 onion
butter
5 cloves
3 allspice berries
1 tsp salt
1–2 tbs vinegar
2 tbs redcurrant jelly

Rinse the cabbage and the apples. Core the apples. Peel the onion.

Cut the cabbage into strips and remove stalk. Cut onion and apples into wedges.

Heat a little butter in a saucepan. Fry cabbage and onion.

Add apples, spices, salt, vinegar, and jelly. Cover and simmer for 40–50 min. Stir from time to time. Check seasoning and add more spices if needed.

Serve with ham, spareribs, or turkey.

Browned Cabbage   4–6 servings

1 cabbage, about 1.5 kg/3 ⅓ lb
butter
1–2 tbs treacle (molasses)
400–500 ml/14–18 fl oz/1 ¼-good 2 cups stock
salt

Rinse the cabbage, cut it into strips, and remove the stalk.

Heat some butter in a heavy-bottomed pot. Brown the cabbage, a little at a time.

Return the cabbage to the pot. Pour on the treacle. Moisten with stock (from the ham, or ordinary stock). Cover and cook on low heat for about 1 hour. Stir from time to time and add more stock if needed. Season with additional salt and treacle if needed.

Serve with ham or sausages.

Cabbage Salad   4 servings

1 wedge of cabbage, about 300 g/10 oz
2 apples
1–2 pickled cucumbers

Sour-cream Sauce:
150–200 ml/5–7 fl oz/⅔– ¾ cup soured cream
1 tbs prepared mustard
¼ tsp salt
¼ tsp white or black pepper

Rinse the cabbage and cut it into very fine strips. Peel the apple (optional) and core. Dice apples and cucumbers finely.

Mix cabbage, apples, and cucumbers in a salad bowl.

Season the soured cream with mustard, salt, and pepper.

Serve the salad with the sauce handed separately.

Red Cabbage Salad   4 servings

½ leek
1 wedge red cabbage, about 300 g/10 oz
1 orange

Rinse leek and cabbage and cut into fine strips. Peel the orange and cut into pieces. Mix all together in a salad bowl.

Rice Porridge 4 servings

Risgrynsgröt

180 g/6⅓ oz/good ¾ cup round-grained rice
300 ml/½ pt/1¼ cups water
1 tsp salt
1 tbs butter
700–800 ml/1¼-scant 1½ pts/3–3⅓ cups milk
about 1 tbs sugar

Bring the water to the boil with salt and butter. Add the rice, cover, and simmer on low heat, until the water has been absorbed, about 10 min. Thin with the milk and bring back to the boiling point. Cover the saucepan and turn off the heat. Leave to cook on the remaining heat. The rice will swell and absorb the milk, and as the heat is very low, the porridge will not burn. If you have a gas-cooker, let the porridge simmer for about 10 min. with the milk. Then place the saucepan on a wooden carving board. The porridge will be cooked after 30–40 min.
Season with sugar. If you wish, you may add a pat of butter and one single almond (blanched and skinned) just before serving.
Serve with milk, ground cinnamon, and sugar (optional).

Rice porridge is the traditional dessert on Christmas Eve. The single, hidden almond is an additional pleasure; whoever finds it will get married within the coming year. Nowadays many Swedes find the rice porridge too heavy. As an alternative they choose the following recipe.

Rice à la Malta 4 servings

Ris à la Malta

180 g/6⅓ oz/good ¾ cup round-grained rice
500 ml/18 fl oz/good 2 cups water
½ tsp salt

200 ml/7 fl oz/good ¾ cup whipping cream
1 tbs sugar
1 tbs vanilline sugar or 2 tsp vanilla extract

Bring the water to the boil with the salt. Add the rice, cover, and simmer on low heat for about 25 min.
Rinse the rice with cold water. Drain and leave to cool.
Whip the cream. Fold it gently into the rice. Season with sugar and vanilline sugar or vanilla extract.
Serve with lightly sweetened raspberries or an orange salad (orange slices sprinkled with sugar).

Mulled Wine

Vinglögg

1 bottle simple red wine, 75 cl
½ bottle port, 33 cl
2 cinnamon sticks
12–15 cardamom seeds
dried orange peel
45–65 g/1½–2⅓ oz/¼–⅓ cup sugar

To serve:
100 g/3½ oz almonds, blanched and skinned
120 g/4¼ oz/good ¾ cup raisins

Mix wine, port, and spices. If possible, let the mixture stand overnight. Heat the wine gently on low heat. It must not be allowed to boil. Season with sugar.
Strain off the spices. Pour the mulled wine into a saucepan. Place the saucepan on a hotplate to keep warm.
Serve in small cups with almonds and raisins.

Variation: *Non-alcoholic* glögg   *Alkoholfri glögg*

Mix 2 parts blackcurrant juice and 1 part apple juice. Heat with the spices as described above. Omit the sugar.
Serve as described above.

Mumma

2 bottles of dark ale, 33 cl/½ pt each
2 bottles of porter, 33 cl/½ pt each
1 bottle of Sprite or 7-up, 33 cl/½ pt
about 50 ml/1¾ fl oz/scant ¼ cup
   Madeira

This is a popular Christmas beverage, originally a kind of beer, drunk already during the 15th century. Nowadays the name is used for a mixture of different kinds of beer with a sweet carbonated drink added.

Mix all together in a large jug. Pour gently along the side of the jug in order to preserve the carbon dioxide.
Serve at once, well chilled.

Home-made Mustard

Hemlagad senap

40 g/1½ oz/scant ¼ cup mustard
   powder
2 tbs flour
75 ml/2⅔ fl oz/⅓ cup boiling water
¼ tsp salt
2–3 tbs sugar
2 tbs wine vinegar
whipping cream or soured cream

Mix mustard powder and flour. Add the boiling water and beat with a fork until the mixture is smooth. Set aside to rest for 10 min.
Season with salt, sugar, and vinegar.
Just before serving, mix in a little whipping cream or soured cream.

EASTER

At Easter most Swedes are looking forward to spring. Birchbranches with tender green leaves are decorating the homes. On the menu eggs have a prominent position, both on their own and in combination with for instance pickled herrings. Apart from the egg there are few traditional dishes associated with Easter. A leg of lamb is served on Easter Sunday in many homes; various salmon dishes are popular in other families. The traditional Easter eggs are served lightly boiled, soft-boiled, or hard-boiled according to your own taste.

Eggs with Spinach 4 servings

Ägg på spenatbädd

4 hard-boiled or soft-boiled eggs
2 tbs butter
1½ tbs flour
150 ml/¼ pt/⅔ cup milk or cream
1 packet frozen chopped spinach, about
   375 g/13 oz
1 tsp salt
¼ tsp white or black pepper
chopped chives

Peel the eggs and cut them in halves. Melt the butter in a saucepan. Blend in the flour. Thin with milk or cream. Add the spinach and let it thaw in the sauce on low heat. Season with salt and pepper. Turn the spinach on to a serving dish and arrange the egg-halves on top. Sprinkle with chives.

Matjes Herring with Chopped Eggs   4 servings   *Matjessill med äggfräs*

4 fillets of matjes herring
3 hard-boiled eggs
2 onions, preferably red ones
50 g/1¾ oz/scant ¼ cup butter

Drain the herring fillets. Cut them in pieces and arrange on a serving dish.
Peel and chop the eggs. Peel and finely chop the onions. Arrange eggs and onions on top of the herrings.
Lightly brown the butter. Pour it hot over the herrings.
Serve at once with boiled potatoes.

Anchovies with Eggs   4 servings   *Ansjovisfat med ägg*

1 tin (appr. 100 g/3½ oz) filleted Swed-
*   ish anchovies or 2 tins of anchovies in*
*   oil*
3 hard-boiled eggs
50 ml/3 rounded tbs chopped chives
200 ml/7 fl oz/good ¾ cup soured
*   cream*
¼ tsp salt
¼ tsp white or black pepper

Drain the anchovy fillets and chop them coarsely. Peel and chop the eggs. Arrange anchovies, eggs, and chives in rows on a serving dish. Season the soured cream with salt and pepper. Hand the cream separately.

Sunny Salad   4 servings   *Solöga*

1 tin (appr. 100 g/3½ oz) Swedish
*   anchovy fillets*
50 ml/3 rounded tbs capers
1 medium-sized onion
200 ml/7 fl oz/good ¾ cup chopped
*   pickled beetroots*
4 raw egg yolks

Drain anchovy fillets and capers. Chop the anchovies. Peel and finely chop the onion. Arrange the ingredients in concentric circles on four small plates. Start by making a small ring of anchovies in the middle of each plate. Continue with capers, onions, and, on the outside, beetroots. Finally, place a raw egg yolk gently in the middle of each plate.

Easter lunch. In many Swedish homes the Easter eggs are painted, a popular pastime for the kids.

Salmon Pudding is served in many homes on God Friday.

Salmon Pudding 4 servings

Laxpudding

200 g / 7 oz lightly salted salmon
8–10 cold boiled potatoes
4 eggs
400 ml / 14 fl oz / 1⅔ cups milk
¼ tsp white or black pepper

To serve:
100 g / 3½ oz / scant ½ cup butter
50 ml / 3 rounded tbs finely chopped dill

Cut the fish into strips. (If it is very salty it should be soaked overnight in a mixture of milk and water.) Slice the potatoes thinly. Arrange potatoes and salmon in alternate layers in a buttered ovenproof dish. Beat eggs, milk, and pepper together and pour into the dish.

Bake in a 200°C / 400°F oven, until the batter is set, about 35 min. Melt the butter and mix it with the dill.

Serve the pudding with the butter handed separately.

Salmon Pie 6 servings

1 kg/2¼ lb salmon, fresh or frozen
water
2 tsp salt per litre/1¾ pts/4¼ cups water
8 white peppercorns
dill sprigs
1 lemon wedge

160 g/5⅔ oz/good ¾ cup long-grained
  rice

100 ml/3½ fl oz/scant ½ cup finely
  chopped dill

For the crust:
240 g/8½ oz/1⅔ cups plain flour
200 g/7 oz/scant cup butter
50 ml/1¾ fl oz/scant ¼ cup water

1 egg

Sauce:
300 ml/½ pt/1¼ cups soured cream
1 tbs tomato purée
50 ml/3 rounded tbs finely chopped dill
¼ tsp salt
¼ tsp white or black pepper

Clean and rinse the fish, but leave skin and bones. Place the fish in a saucepan. Measure the water and pour in enough to cover the fish. Add salt, pepper, dill sprigs, and lemon. Cover and simmer on low heat for 20–30 min., depending on the thickness of the fish. Set aside to cool in the stock.

Boil the rice according to the instructions on the packet. Set aside to cool.

Put flour and butter on the pastry board. Rub the butter into the flour until the mixture is crumbly. Add the water and mix quickly with your hands to a dough. Chill for about 30 min. Skin and bone the fish.

Roll out a little less than half of the pastry into a thin oval and place it on a buttered baking sheet. Distribute salmon, rice, and dill over the pastry. Roll out the remaining pastry (keep a little aside for decoration) and place it on top of the filling. Press down the edges with a fork. Decorate with "fins" made from the left-over pastry. Brush the top with beaten egg.

Bake in a 225°C/435°F oven for about 30 min.

Sauce: Mix soured cream, tomato purée and dill. Season with salt and pepper.

Serve the pie with the sauce and a green salad.

Easter Cake appr. 8 servings

400 g/14 oz almond paste
4 eggs
50 ml/1¾ fl oz/scant ¼ cup orange juice

To decorate:
100 g/3½ oz plain dark cooking
  chocolate
marcipan chickens or mandarin
  segments

Grate the almond paste coarsely. Mix almond paste, eggs, and orange juice. Stir vigorously, using for instance an electric beater, until you have a light and fluffy mixture.

Turn into a buttered and floured plain tin.

Bake in a 200°C/400°F oven, until nicely browned and done, about 30 min.

Unmould the cake.

Break the chocolate into pieces and put them on the hot cake.

Cover with the inverted tin. After a while the chocolate has melted and you can spread it with a knife. Leave the cake to cool.

Decorate with little marzipan chickens or well-drained tinned mandarin segments.

Egg-nog one serving

1–2 egg yolks
1 tbs icing (confectionary) sugar
200 ml/7 fl oz/good ¾ cup orange juice
or 150 ml/¼ pt/⅔ cup hot water
2–3 tbs brandy

Beat egg yolks and sugar with a fork in a tall glass until very light and fluffy. (If you make several servings at the same time, you may use an electric beater.)

Add orange juice or hot water and brandy.

MIDSUMMER

On Midsummer's Eve many Swedes are dancing round the maypole. Lunch on Midsummer's Day is often eaten out-of-doors and consists of matjes herring with new potatoes and soured cream.

Matjes Herring 4 servings

Matjessill

2–4 fillets of Matjes Herring (a sweet-
  pickled herring, which is to be found
  in many delicatessen shops)
100 ml/3½ fl oz/scant ½ cup finely
  chopped chives
200 ml/7 fl oz/good ¾ cup soured
  cream

Cut the herring fillets in pieces. Arrange on a serving dish. Surround with chopped chives.

Serve with soured cream, boiled new potatoes, and tomatoes.

Marinated Salmon 6 servings

1 kg/2¼ lb salmon (fresh or frozen)
45 g/1½ oz/scant ¼ cup sugar
65 g/2⅓ oz/scant ¼ cup salt
1 tbs crushed white peppercorns
1 bunch dill

Sauce:
50 ml/3½ fl oz/scant ¼ cup mustard
  (Swedish, German, or Dijon)
1–2 tbs sugar
¼ tsp salt
2 tbs vinegar
100 ml/3½ fl oz/scant ½ cup salad oil
50 ml/3 rounded tbs finely chopped dill

Partly thaw the salmon if it is frozen. Cut into two boneless fillets. Leave the skin on. Dry the fillets on paper towels, but do not rinse them.

Mix sugar, salt, and pepper. Rinse the dill, drain, and chop roughly.

Scatter a little of the spice mixture and dill on a large sheet of aluminium foil and place one of the fillets on it, skinside down.

Sprinkle with dill and spices. Put the other fillet on top, turned so that its thick, fleshy part rests on the thin part of the lower fillet. Sprinkle with the rest of the spice mixture and dill.

Fold up the foil into a tight package. Place in a plastic bag and tie up. Refrigerate for 48 hours, turning once.

Scrape away dill and spices. Cut the fillets into thin skinless slices on the bias.

Sauce: Mix mustard, sugar, salt, and vinegar. Add the oil drop by drop while stirring vigorously. The sauce should be thick and smooth. Add the dill. Season with salt and pepper if needed. Serve the salmon with the sauce, lemon wedges, toast, and butter.

It may also be served with Potatoes in White Sauce (see page 52).

Perch, Roasted in the Embers 4 servings

1 kg/2¼ lb perch
2 tsp salt
¼ tsp white or black pepper

Stuffing:
4 tbs butter
50 ml/3 rounded tbs each finely chop-
  ped dill and parsley
1 tbs chopped chives

Clean and rinse the fish carefully. Sprinkle with salt and pepper outside and inside. Mix butter and green herbs. Stuff the fish with the herb butter.

Place each fish on a buttered piece of aluminium foil and fold into tight packets. Grill the fish packets on charcoal, 8–12 min. each side, depending on the thickness of the fish.

Serve the perch in their packets with boiled new potatoes, buttered nettles or spinach, and a tomato salad.

A typical Lunchtable on Midsummer's Day.

Rainbow Trout in Aspic 4 servings

750 g/1⅔ lb rainbow trout

Court-bouillon:
1 l/1¾ pts/4¼ cups water
1 tbs salt
5 white peppercorns
2 tsp vinegar or lemon juice
1 small onion or 1 small leek
dill and parsley sprigs

Aspic:
800 ml/scant 1½ pts/3⅓ cups fish stock
1⅓ tbs plain unsweetened powdered
  gelatine

Garnish:
2 hard-boiled eggs
about 75 g/2½ oz shelled prawns
  (shrimps) (about 200 g/7 oz prawns
  in their shells)
1 piece of fresh cucumber
dill

Sour-cream Sauce:
200 ml/7 fl oz/good ¾ cup soured
  cream
2 tbs prepared mustard
50 ml/3 rounded tbs chopped dill
¼ tsp salt
¼ tsp white or black pepper

Clean and rinse the fish. Bring the water to the boil with salt, peppercorns, vinegar or lemon juice, the peeled onion or leek cut in pieces, dill and parsley. Boil for 5 min. Add the fish, cover, and poach on very low heat for 8–10 min. Leave the fish to cool in the stock.

Take out the fish and remove skin and bones. Cut the fish into pieces.

Strain the stock, for instance through a paper filter (coffee filter).

Measure out 800 ml (scant 1½ pts/3⅓ cups) stock and pour into a saucepan.

Soften the gelatine in 3–4 tbs of the stock. When softened, add it to the rest of the stock and heat, while stirring. Allow to cool, but not to set.

Use one large mould or small individual moulds. Pour a thin layer of aspic into the mould and let it set. Arrange fish, egg slices, prawns, thin slices of cucumber, and small sprigs of dill in the mould. Pour in the rest of the aspic and leave to set in a cold place.

Dip the mould into hot water and turn out the aspic. If there is any left-over garnish, use it to decorate.

Mix soured cream, mustard, and dill. Season with salt and pepper.

Serve the aspic with the sauce, boiled new potatoes, and a green salad.

Strawberry Cake appr. 12 servings

3 eggs
130 g/4½ oz/⅔ cup sugar
120 g/4¼ oz/good ¾ cup flour
1 tsp baking powder

Filling and decoration:
300 ml/½ pt/1¼ cups whipping cream
500–750 g/1–1⅔ lb fresh strawberries

Whip eggs and sugar until very light and fluffy. Sift the flour with the baking powder and fold it into the egg-mixture. Turn into a buttered and floured 2 l (3½ pts/8 cups) mould. Bake in a 175°C/350°F oven for about 35 min. Turn out the cake and leave to cool. Cut the cake horisontally into two or three layers.

Whip the cream. Slice half of the strawberries or mash them. Sweeten to taste. Fill the cake with the strawberries and a little of the cream. Decorate with the rest of the cream and berries.

The first Swedish strawberries appear just in time for Midsummer.

Meringue Cake   10–12 servings

Chocolate cake:
125 g/4½ oz/good ½ cup butter
85 g/3 oz/scant ½ cup sugar
2 egg yolks
100 ml/3½ fl oz/scant ½ cup milk
90 g/good 3 oz/⅔ cup flour
2 tsp baking powder
2 tbs cocoa powder

Meringue:
2 egg whites
150 g/5⅓ oz/¾ cup sugar
1 tsp vanilline sugar or ½ tsp vanilla
   extract
50 ml/3 rounded tbs flaked almonds

Filling:
300 ml/½ pt/1¼ cup whipping cream

Cream butter and sugar until very light. Stir in the egg yolks, one at a time. Add the milk.

Sift flour, baking powder, and cocoa powder together and fold it into the mixture.

Beat the egg whites until stiff. Fold in sugar and vanilline sugar or vanilla extract.

Line a large rectangular tin with baking paper. Brush the paper with a little oil.

Spread the chocolate mixture on the baking paper. Spread the meringue on top.

Sprinkle with the almond flakes.

Bake in a 175°C/350°F oven for about 20 min.

Turn out the cake on to a cake rack. Pull off the paper. Reverse the cake and allow to cool.

Whip the cream.

Cut the cake into halves along the middle. Spread the whipped cream on one of the halves and put the other half on top.

CRAYFISH AND FERMENTED BALTIC HERRING

Crayfish and fermented herring are seasonal dishes, both belonging to the autumn. The crayfish season starts on 8th August, and on that day most Swedish restaurants and many private homes arrange crayfish parties. Swedish crayfish have now become too scarce to meet the ever-increasing demand, and so frozen crayfish, cooked in the Swedish way are imported from other countries.

Fermented herring is a very old Swedish dish, which originated in the northern part of the country. The herrings were packed into barrels with weak brine and left in the sun to ferment. Nowadays fermented herring is available tinned, in supermarkets all over Sweden.

The *surströmming* season opens in late August. To make a traditional *surströmming* party you need, of course, a tin of fermented herrings (open it out-of-doors or inside a plastic bag in the kitchen, because the juice may squirt and the smell is very strong for uninitiated noses).

Boiled Crayfish, a Meringue Cake and a Cheese Pie.

Boiled Crayfish 3–4 servings   *Kokta kräftor*

1 kg/2¼ lb live crayfish

Court-bouillon:
2 l/3½ pts/8½ cups water
190 g/6½ oz/⅔ cup salt
2 sugar lumps
*100 ml/3½ fl oz/scant ½ cup lager
    (optional)*
a generous quantity of dill heads

Check that all the crayfish are alive.
Heat water, salt, sugar, and optional lager in a large pot.
Add half of the dill heads. Bring to a rolling boil. Add the crayfish and check that they are well covered by the court-bouillon. Cover and boil briskly for 8–10 min.
Remove the dill heads and replace them with fresh ones. Cool the crayfish in their court-bouillon as quickly as possible, for instance by placing the pot in cold water. Change the cooling water frequently. Refrigerate the crayfish in their cold court-bouillon for 24 hours before serving.

Variation: *Boiled Frozen Crayfish*   *Kokta frysta kräftor*

Follow the master recipe, but use only 90 g (good 3 oz/⅓ cup) salt. Bring the water to the boil with salt, sugar, and optional lager. Add the dill heads. Set aside to cool.
Thaw frozen crayfish according to the instructions on the packet, until they can be separated. Place the crayfish in the cold court-bouillon. Leave in a cold place for 24 hours.
Serve the crayfish with bread, butter, and a spicy, wellripened cheese.

August Dessert 4 servings

Augustidessert

1 melon, about 750 g/1⅔ lb
250 g/9 oz fresh raspberries or corres-
ponding quantity frozen ones
250 g/9 oz red- or blackcurrants (stalks
removed)
2 tbs icing (confectionary) sugar
2 tbs liquor, eg. Cointreau (optional)

Cut a thin slice off the bottom of the melon, so that it can stand. Cut off the top to form a lid. Remove the seeds with a spoon. Scoop out most of the pulp, taking care not to break the skin. Dice the pulp.

Arrange the diced melon, raspberries, red- or black-currants, and icing sugar in alternate layers in the melon. Pour in the optional liquor. Replace the lid. Chill the melon until serving.

Apart from the herrings you need boiled potatoes, Soft or Crisp Flatbread (see page 88), Chopped onion, and a spicy cheese. Beer (and snaps) go excellently with fermented herring, but some Swedes prefer milk.

MARTINMAS

St. Martin's Day is celebrated, mainly in the southern part of Sweden, on the 10th November. The traditional dinner is based on the goose. It starts with a spicy Black Soup, made with goose blood and goose stock. The soup is garnished with pieces of a sausage made with the goose liver. The main course is the goose itself, stuffed with apples and prunes. The sweet is often a *spettekaka* (pyramid cake), another Scanian speciality.

Black Soup   10–12 servings   *Svartsoppa*

*500–600 ml/18–21 fl oz/2–2½ cups
   blood from goose or pig
60 g/2 oz/scant ½ cup flour
2.5 l/4½ pts/2⅔ quarts stock, made with
   the goose giblets (heart, gizzard, wing
   tips, and neck)
water
1½ tsp salt per litre/1¾ pts/4¼ cups
   water*

*3–4 tsp salt
3–4 tbs sugar
2 tbs vinegar
½ tsp white pepper
½ tsp ground ginger
½ tsp ground cloves
about 2 tbs brandy
100–200 ml/3½–7 fl oz/½–¾ cup
   sherry
100–200 ml/3½–7 fl oz/½–¾ cup cooking liquid from apples and prunes*

Place the goose giblets in salted water and boil until tender, about 1½ hours.
Strain the blood. Beat in the flour.
Bring the stock to the boil. Beat in the blood mixture.
Simmer on very low heat, stirring continously for 7–8 min.
Remove from the heat and season with salt, sugar, vinegar, spices, brandy, sherry, and cooking liquid from the fruit.
Serve with goose liver sausage, pieces of giblets, boiled apple slices, and prunes.

The soup may be prepared a day in advance; it will bring out the fine spicy flavour. Stir continously while reheating, to prevent the soup from curdling.

Goose Liver Sausage   10–12 servings   *Gåsleverkorv*

*80 g/2¾ oz/scant ½ cup rice
500 ml/18 fl oz/good 2 cups milk
1 goose liver
100 g/3½ oz calf's liver
1 tbs finely chopped, fried onion
30 g/1 oz/scant ¼ cup raisins
1 tbs treacle (molasses)
1½ tsp salt
¼ tsp white pepper
¼ tsp marjoram
1 egg
a length of intestine (soaked) or the neck
   skin from the goose
water
2 tsp salt per litre/1¾ pts/4¼ cups water*

Boil the rice with the milk for about 15 min. Mince or finely chop the liver. Mix all the ingredients together.
Stuff an intestine or the goose's neck skin with the mixture.
Tie up the ends. Put the sausage in lightly salted water and simmer on low heat for about 45 min.
Leave to cool. Cut the sausage into slices and serve with the black soup.

Roast Goose.

Roast Goose   10–12 servings

1 goose, 4–5 kg/9–11 lb
1 lemon
1–1½ tbs salt
½–¾ tsp white or black pepper

Stuffing:
4–5 apples
1 packet stoned prunes, about 250 g/
*   9 oz*

Thaw the goose according to the instructions on the package. Remove neck and giblets and boil them for the soup. Rub the goose with lemon inside and outside. Season with salt and pepper. Quarter and core the apples. Stuff the goose with the apples and the prunes. Truss up the bird with cotton string.

Place the goose on its side on a rack in a roasting pan.

Roast in a 175°C/350°F oven. After about 40 min., turn the goose on to the other side. After another 40 min., turn it breast upwards. Allow a total roasting time of 1¾–2½ hours. Test by piercing the thickest part of the leg with a fork or a skewer. Remove the trussing strings. Carve the goose. Loosen the breast meat and cut it into diagonal slices. Cut off the legs and slice their upper parts.

Serve with boiled or browned potatoes, boiled apple halves filled with redcurrant jelly, or prunes, and red cabbage or Brussels sprouts.

The pyramid cake is a Scanian cake, which can be made in various sizes. (Fomerly the size of a pyramid cake used to be specified in scores of eggs.) A pyramid cake is often served at big feasts as for instance weddings, but it is also frequently served at the traditional goose dinner. A fine egg and sugar mixture is piped on to a metal cone, which is slowly turning over an open fire.

Index